NIGERIA'S THIRD REPUBLIC:

THE PROBLEMS AND PROSPECTS OF POLITICAL TRANSITION TO CIVIL RULE

NIGERIA'S THIRD REPUBLIC:

THE PROBLEMS AND PROSPECTS OF POLITICAL TRANSITION TO CIVIL RULE

EDITED BY

BAMIDELE A. OJO

NOVA SCIENCE PUBLISHERS, INC.
Commack, New York
1998

Editorial Production: Susan Boriotti
Office Manager: Annette Hellinger
Graphics: Frank Grucci and John T'Lustachowski
Information Editor: Tatiana Shohov
Book Production: Donna Dennis, Patrick Davin, Christine Mathosian, Tammy Sauter and Diane Sharp
Circulation: Maryanne Schmidt
Marketing/Sales: Cathy DeGregory

Library of Congress Cataloging-in-Publication Data

Nigeria's Third Republic : the problems and prospects of political transition to civil rule / Bamidele A. Ojo (ed.).
p. cm.
Includes bibliographical references and index.
ISBN 1-56072-580-X
1. Civil-military relations—Nigeria. 2. Nigeria—Politics and government—1984- 3. Nigeria—Economic policy. I. Ojo, Bamidele A.
JQ3086.C58N56 1998 98-28665
320.9669—dc21 CIP

6080 Jericho Turnpike, Suite 207
Commack, New York 11725
Tele. 516-499-3103 Fax 516-499-3146
e-mail: Novascience@earthlink.net
e-mail: Novascil@aol.com
Web Site: http://www.nexusworld.com/nova

Printed in the United States of America

CONTENTS

PREFACE

This is a collection of works on political transition to civil rule in Nigeria. Each of the contributors examines the socio-political and economic ramification of the transfer of power to an elected civilian administration.

The year 1992, was important to the research because of the promised transition by Ibrahim Babangida (he later revised the transition program and extended his administration for another year and then annulled the election of June 12, 1993 while instituting an interim government which later was ousted by his Defense Chief, Sanni Abacha - he himself has promised a transition to democratic governance by the year 1998).

The introduction brings us up to speed with the transition program in Nigeria. While in the first chapter, Jubrin Ibrahim, examine the relationship between the state, capital accumulation democratic forces and the politics of transition in Nigeria.

In chapter two, Sylvester Fajoyomi, examines the importance of grass-root mobilization in the political process in Nigeria and how it was reflected in the process of Constitutional development. In the third chapter, Ojo examines the military and the politics of political transition in Nigeria. He identifies the characteristic political manipulation by the military and the attempt to hold on to power despite demand for civilian democratic rule.

The fourth chapter by Adepoju Adeleke, examines the core problems of Nigerian economic management while identifying alternatives for effective management of the Nigerian economy in the Third Republic.

In the fifth chapter, Remi Ajibewa critically study the foreign policy options of the next civilian administration taking cognizance of the changing world order.

Chapter six, by Philemon Oyewole highlights the problems of the present Nigerian marketing system and propose policy alternative for sustaining economic growth. While in chapter seven, Bamidele Ojo, relates the problem of Military intervention to the question of national integration. He observes that the military has been a disintegrative rather than an integrative force in Nigeria.

In the last chapter, Pita Agbese and Julius Ihonvbere, documents the place and role of corruption in both the adjustment and political transition program.

Brief Biography of the Contributors

Adebayo Adeleke

Formerly a lecturer in Economics at the University of Ibadan, Nigeria, Dr. Adepoju holds a BS degree in economics, an MBA, MS and Ph.D. in Management. He did his doctoral research at the University of Aix-Marseille III in France. He is currently a management consultant at the International labor Organization office in Lagos, Nigeria.

Pita Agbese

Dr. Agbese is currently a Professor of African Politics at the Northern Iowa University.

Aderemi Ajibewa

He is currently teaching at the University of Malaysia and formerly a lecturer in International relations at the Obafemi Awolowo University, Ile-Ife, Nigeria. Aderemi also holds a BS [Political science][University of Ibadan], an MS in International relations [Obafemi Awolowo University] and was a British Airways Scholar [1989-1990] at the university of Sussex with a PhD from the University of Manchester in England. He has published extensively on African Politics.

SYLVESTER FAJOYOMI

Dr Fajoyomi holds a doctorate from the Institute of Political Studies, Center for Local Government studies at the University of Bordeaux, France. He also holds a BS in Political Science and an MS in Local Government Studies from Obafemi Awolowo University. He is currently teaching at the University of Lagos, Nigeria.

JULIUS IHONVBERE

Dr. Ihonvbere is a Professor of African Politics at the University of Texas at Austin. He has published extensively on Nigerian, African and Third World politics. He is the author of many award winning books on contemporary Nigerian and African politics.

JIBRIN IBRAHIM

Jibo, graduated from Amadu Bello University and did his doctorate at the University of Bordeaux. France. He currently teaches politics at the Amadu Bello University, in Kaduna, Nigeria. Dr Ibrahim, has published extensively on Nigerian politics.

BAMIDELE A. OJO

Dr Ojo graduated with an Mphil and Ph.D. from the Institute of Political studies, Center for African studies, University of Bordeaux, France. He holds a BS in Political Science, MS in International relations [University of Ife, Nigeria] LLM in International Law [University of Nottingham, England].An Associate Member of the Institute for International Humanitarian Law [San Remo, Italy], Dr Ojo, an Associate Professor of Political Science, teaches Politics and African Studies at the School of Political and International Studies, Fairleigh Dickinson University, Teaneck, New Jersey. Dr. Ojo has published extensively on African

Politics and International relations/Law. He is the author of Human Rights In a New World Order: Universality, Acceptability and Human Diversity (New York: Nova Science Publishers, May 1997).

PHILEMON O. OYEWOLE

Dr Oyewole is an Assistant Professor of Marketing at Howard University, Washington D.C. and holds the following degrees: BS in Demography and Social statistics and an MBA, [Obafemi Awolowo University, Nigeria] an Mphil and PhD in Marketing from the University of Aix-Maiseille III, France. He is also a consultant at the World Bank. He has published in many journals.

Chapter One

THE STATE, ACCUMULATION AND DEMOCRATIC FORCES IN NIGERIA

Jibrin Ibrahim*

Nigeria was one of the new countries in Africa with a significant reputation of protecting civil liberties. In fact, one could talk of a certain democratic tradition in the country's political culture. This assertion was without doubt a paradoxical one, especially as the military regimes conducted Nigerian affairs during 28 of its 38 years of independence. The military was constrained until recently to bottled up their authoritarian habits and conduct the nation's affairs as civilians and with civilians, more or less guided by a constitution.

The first task of a military regime after a coup d'état is to suspend the constitution, but then, only the sections of the constitution that regulates partisan politics are usually suspended while the other sections, especially those that defines the functions and powers of the judiciary and the human rights clause are left to function - that is until recently - meaning since 1988.

In spite of the democratic tradition in Nigeria, analysts from both the developmentalist and from the dependency schools, have failed to properly conceptualize and analyze Nigerian democracy (Bangura). Two things have usually been ignored. First, that there is a rich but contradictory democratic

---

* Paper presented at the AKUT Conference on "When Does Democracy Make Sense", at the University of Uppsala. (October 26-28, 1989)

tradition embedded in Nigerian civil society and secondly the pattern of capital accumulation in the country is dysfunctional if not destructive of this democratic tradition. The democratic tradition in' civil society is organized around a relatively fierce press(a press that has suffered tremendous prosecution in the last few years), a fairly developed judicial system, a strong culture of union struggle and a political system based upon disparate centers of power and governed by "checks and balances" that has prevented the rise of tyrannical or even oligarchic regimes at the national level[This assertion is untrue today because of the authoritarian nature of the Nigerian military and the politicization of the judiciary and suppression of opposition and abuse of human rights since the Babangida regime [Editors' note].

In spite of these democratic assets, the history of liberal democratic regimes in Nigeria has been anything but glorious. Elections, a central element of the democratic process, have usually been rigged by parties in power and marked by political violence. Even press freedom and the independence of the judiciary have often been compromised by governmental abuse of power.

In addition to these limitations, the reckless manner in which the nascent bourgeoisie in Nigeria is engaged In a process of primitive accumulation of capital and the Hobbesian struggle for power which results from the process is pushing Nigerian politics towards increased violence, intolerance and arbitrariness, elements that tend to erode democratic political culture. it would seem that the near total dependence of the Nigerian bourgeoisie on state resources has blown the importance of state power out all proportions. The state becomes 'too important' to be left to 'capricious' democratic forces.

The present conjuncture is therefore a very difficult *one* for Nigerian democracy. That there are democratic assets is, incontestable, but then these assets have limitations and they are confronted with dangers. To understand the present conjecture, the colonial aspects of the Nigerian political system must be put in perspective.

I: The British Tradition

During the years of 'self Government' - 1957 to 1960 and the years of the 'First Republic' - 1960 to 1965 the situation was clear, or so it seemed. Nigeria' had inherited the British tradition of liberal democracy known as the Westminster model. The Prime Minister of the epoch, Abubakar Tafawa Balewa while commenting on the 'cordial relations' between Nigeria and Great Britain explained that "Their system of democratic government has now become part of our own heritage and we should we wise to maintain our institutions on the British model". (Oyovbaire 1987: 4)

What then was this British model? It was certainly not the type of profound democratic political culture organized around a centralized administration that is found in the United Kingdom of Her Majesty. It was a system of 'indirect rule' established by Lord Lugard, the British colonial administrator. It was based on a policy of non-centralized administration or separate government for 'different peoples'. This policy led to the evolution of certain structures and institutions which to a certain extent still characterize contemporary Nigerian State.

A. Structures

The basic principle of 'Indirect Rule' - was 'divide and rule'. In the Emirates of Northern Nigeria and in the Yoruba kingdoms of the south west, indigenous political structures were retained and often reinforced by the colonial administration as the primary level of government, while in the South East as well as among some of the acephalous 'Middle Belt' societies, a new order of colonial chiefs known as 'warrant chiefs' was imposed. The system of 'Indirect Rule' had a profound impact on the evolution of Nigerian elite. In the North, traditional elites were fully involved in the administration of British imperialism thanks to the system of 'Native Administration' (NA) and were therefore allies of the Crown.

Secondly, they had a pact with Lord Lugard to keep Christian missionaries and by extension, western education, out of the Emirates. The result was that the pace of development of western education in the Muslim part of the North was very slow and the few that "ere chosen for the western schools were all employed in the NA. Thus, the totality of the elite in the Muslim North collaborated with colonialism and had a stake in it.

In the other parts of the country, Christian missionaries were given full freedom for proselytization and virtually exclusive control of Western education. It resulted in a fairly rapid evolution of a Western educated elite, to the detriment of traditional ruling elite. The new elite however had very limited chances of integrating into the upper echelons of the civil service even when they had high levels of education. With their high education and the frustrations of being kept out, they naturally drifted into political agitation and adversary journalism, an argument that will be development below.

In the North, the British evolved a selection process to create a new educated elite to replace, or rather to work with, the emirate aristocracy. Starting with the Kano 'Nassarawa' school in 1909, two new ones came up in 1913 at Katsina and Sokoto, and another in Maiduguri in 1915. In 1922 Katsina College (later Barewa College) was established and it became the base for the creation of northern, Muslim and conservative leaders that later grew into what is widely known as the 'Northern Oligarchy'. (Ibrahim 1987) The Nigerian democratic game therefore took off with these divided elite as actors whose theater was also to be composed of institutions of division.

B. Institutions

Nigeria was not colonized as a unified British territory. It was composed of three separate units - the Colony of Lagos and the two Protectorates of Northern and Southern Nigeria, each administered separately. In 1914, the three units were united to constitute the colony of Nigeria with an internal division between the North and the South which continued to be administered separately. In 1938 the South was divided into two regions, the West and East. This last division followed the British 'discovery' of a Yoruba and Benin political tendency halfway between the centralized Northern Emirates and the 'acephalous' political Organization in the East - hence the origins of the tripartite system. This system was formalized with the Richards Constitution of 1946 and five years later, Governor Macpherson's Constitution 'federated the three regions by creating a central assembly in addition to the regional ones and devolving effective executive power to the regionally constituted elite.

The guiding principle of this tripartite Federation was that each Region had a 'majority ethnic group's which was to play the role of the leading actor - in the North the Hausa, in the West the Yoruba, and in the East the Igbo. In fact the whole process of constitution making between 1946 and 1958 was an elaborate bargaining pantomime to find an equilibrium between the three regions or rather between the leading elite of the majority ethnic groups. No wonder the process resulted in the emergence of three major political parties.

In 1944, Herbert Macaulay and his nationalist friends formed the National Council of Nigeria and the Cameroons (NCNC), a nationalists mass-based party composed of trade unions, ethnic associations and youth movements. Following Macaulay's death in 1947, another politician with nationalist credentials, Nnamdi Azikiwe took over the leadership of the party. The pan Nigerian character of the party was compromised a year later with the formation of the Igbo State Union (ISU); an Igbo federation which was soon to take over control of the NCNC.ISU itself was formed in response to the establishment in 1947 of the Egbe Omo Oduduwa, a pan-Yoruba ethnic association, by Awolowo and some of his (anti-Zik) friends. The Egbe was transformed into a political party in 1950, the Action Group (AG).

In the North, the exigencies of the 1951 elections and the challenge posed by the rise of nationalism in the south, precipitated the formation of a pan-northern party, the Northern Peoples Congress, (NPC) from a regional cultural association - Jam'iyyar Mutanen Arewa. From that point on, the tripartite model of the politics of the First Republic was set in the popular imagination. In a near total misreading of Nigerian politics, Richard Joseph in his book "Democracy and prebendal Politics in Nigeria"(1987) argued that the politics of the 2nd Republic was also based purely on the tripolar model.

Nigerian politics is not tripolar, it is tri-tendential. The first tendency is the tripolar one so characteristic of the politics of the First Republic. This resulted from the domination of the political scene by the three major groups already referred to an element we shall return to below. The second tendency is the bipolar one, a weak tendency that is usually expressed during electoral periods.

During the 1964 Federal Elections, political parties regrouped themselves in two blocs. The Government bloc, the Nigerian National Alliance (NNA) was composed of the Northern Peoples Congress (NPC), Nigerian National Democratic Party (NNDP), Mid-west Democratic Front (MDF) and Niger Delta Congress (NDC). The Opposition, United Progressive Grand Alliance (UPGA) was composed of the National Congress of Nigerian Citizens (NCNC), Action Group (AC-) and Northern Progressive Front (NPF) which was itself an alliance of the United Middle Belt Congress(UMBC) and Northern Elements Progressive Union(NEPU).

This regrouping which took the form of progressive/conservative forces actually reflected tactical maneuver of a multiplicity of political group better access to political power and the rewards it brings. That was why the composition of the alliances changed from time to time. The UMBC for example has had alliances at different times with the NPC, AC and NEPU.

During the 1983 elections, this bipolar tendency took the form of Government groups composed of the National Party of Nigeria (NPN) and splinter factions from the five other parties and an Opposition group of the rest known as the Progressive Peoples Alliance (PPA).

After almost thirty years of shifting bipolar alliances, and a concerted effort by the Babangida Administration to institutionalize bipartisan politics bipolarity is one of the tendencies of Nigerian politics even if it hides a more profound multipolar tendency.

Nigeria is not composed of two or three cultural groups but of hundreds of cultural and ethnic groups the majority of which are dominated by the so called majority groups. The third and essential tendency, in Nigerian politics is an multi-polarity which is continuously repressed with imposed bipolarity and or tri-polarity. We have described tendency elsewhere, using contemporary French phraseology as "the politics of variable geometry" (Ibrahim 1988b). None of the three regions of the First Republic represented a historic political bloc. In the East, immediately the Ibo State Union was formed, it was confronted by the lbibio State Union. The anti-Igbo feeling in the Delta was so strong that in February 1966, Major Isaac Boro declared the secession of the 'Niger Delta Peoples Republic' in protest against Igbo leadership and this first formal secession attempt in Nigeria also resulted in the first declared civil war, the now forgotten 12 day war (Boro 1982).

Political differences in the West are more well known and need not be repeated. In the North, many political poles exist, some of which could briefly be mentioned. The dominant pole is rooted in the Sokoto Caliphate zone and it was this group that the British maneuvered to place in power between 1946 and 1951 because they had cooperated so closely in the system of 'Native Administration' (NA). The second pole in the same zone is the radical anti-aristocratic tendency that was expressed by the NEPU/PRP heritage. The third pole is the Bornu tendency expressed in the BYM and to some extent in the GNPP while the fourth one is the Northern minorities tendency expressed in the Northern Nigeria non-

Muslim League formed in 1950 and transformed into the United Middle Belt Peoples Congress in 1953.

All these political divisions were violently repressed by the WAZOBIA[1] domination in the three regions especially as the Westminster Federalism of the First Republic evolved with the center of political power being the regions rather than the center, unlike in the British case. The refusal of the British to create more regions in 1958 when the Willink Commission affirmed that fears of domination of the 'minorities' by the 'majorities' were justified was virtually a disenfranchisement a 45 per cent of the population.

The politics of the First Republic evolved in a contradictory manner with the multi-polar tendency being simultaneously suppressed and supported. In each region, it was suppressed by the Regional Government but then encouraged and supported by the other Regional Governments, hence the elaborate system of shifting national alliances. The domination of political power by the Northern pole meant that a democratic change of Government at the center was virtually impossible for the simple reason that internal regional democracy was impossible.

The Caliphate Oligarchy in control of the NPC could maintain perpetual control of federal power, although it was a minority even in the North, its base, thanks to the principle that the elite of the dominant ethnic group in each region had become the inheritors of political power.

The North, with 54 per cent of official representatives, could always thwart shifting bipolar alliances by destabilizing them.

The evolution of political structures and institutions in Nigeria was not therefore particularly democratic. The system of Native Administration (NA) which left vast powers - police, courts and prisons - in the hands of chiefs was a basic negation of democratic principles. The democratic process itself, gas systematically subverted by the system of WAZOBIA tyranny within the Regions.

Elections were so massively rigged that they became farcical. In spite of these failures, however, the British police of divide and rule which produced a multivariate framework of political structures and institutions prevented the evolution of a unified national oligarchic or sultanic leadership. In addition, the instability of the system and its ingrained 'fears of domination' encouraged the evolution of a culture of struggle for political survival and self assertion. It is an this background that a certain democratic tradition has evolved in Nigerian civil

[1] WAZOBIA - a composite word from the verb to come in the three major languages which represents domination by the majority groups in Nigeria=s popular psyche.

society organized around a relatively free press, a developed Judiciary and a tradition of trade union struggle.

II: Nigerian Democratic Assets and their weaknesses

Citizens of other African countries often talk about the democratic 'success story' of Nigeria being spoilt by its chaos and instability. What is clear is that democracy is an arena of contestation in Nigeria or to put it differently there is a democratic drive embedded in Nigerian civil society. Guy Hermet (1984: 99) has argued that a democratic drive is nourished by contradictory elements - in particular the growth of the expectation for popular participation faced with sociological, suffrage censoring'. In re-popularizing the debate on the future for democracy in Africa, Richard Sklar (1986: 17) has proposed the existence of a 'vital force' that creates an expectation of 'accountability of values' which no coup d'état can kill and that therefore the age of the 'developmental dictatorship' is over. The vital force of Nigerian democracy is seen very clearly in its media of mass communications.

A. The Role of the Mass Media

The Nigerian mass media have a long and rich history. Their origins are rooted in the dialectic between missionary education and colonial administration in Southern Nigeria. The educational program of the missionaries was based essentially on the three R's - reading, writing and arithmetic - to provide the clerks, messengers, interpreters and teachers colonialism needed. Sometimes however, highly educated Nigerians emerged from the system through going abroad to extend their learning and the problem-that arose was that colonial administration was unwilling to accept blacks in the so-called Senior Service.

Even distributive trade and mining were blocked to the emerging African elite. This meant that only law and medicine were left to offer 'honorable' employment to the black elite and those who did not read these two disciplines tended o be pushed towards journalism - the other option.

Journalism developed rapidly because establishing commercial presses was one way of self-employment which had the added advantage of being a political weapon against the exclusionary colonial system. The first newspaper established in Nigeria was Iwe Irohin, a missionary organ produced at Abeokuta from 1859. In 1862 the first agitational newspaper, the Anglo-African was established in Lagos. Its editor, Horace Campbell was a mulatto conscripted into the colonial army from the West Indies. After his army career, he tried commerce but was confronted with colonial racism and commercial blockages, hence his conversion to journalism. Since then, the press developed rapidly as an instrument of political agitation by the educated and frustrated elite that was kept out of the colonial system. The Lagos Weekly Record, for example, complained in 1897 that the most unenviable position of the British West African colonies, the worst feature of which was that the people themselves had little or no voice at all in the administration of their affairs. (cited Omu 1978: 149)

Between 1862 and 1913 these journalist-cum-politicians such as James Davies of the Nigerian Times, John Jackson of Lagos Weekly Times, Sapara Williams of Lagos Weekly Record, and F.D. Morel of the African Mail became the pioneers of the struggle for public liberties as they fought against the excesses of the colonial laws, racial segregation, land alienation and taxes. Alarmed by this tendency, Lord Lugard convinced his Nigerian friend, Sir Kitoye Ajasa to launch a pro-colonial newspaper, the Nigerian Pioneer, which operated from 1914 to 1936. The European Chamber of Commerce in 1925 also launched a pro-colonial newspaper, the Daily Times, the only one from that epoch still in existence. Two tendencies were thus reflected in the press - one conservative and pro-colonial, the other radical and anti-colonial.

The anti-colonial press received a boost in the early 1920s following the formation of the Nigerian National Democratic Party [NNDP] and its newspaper, the Lagos Daily News, and the campaigns (or elections of that period of so-called proto-nationalism. The next phase was the arrival of Nnamdi Azikiwe in 1937 and his 'ELEC-ZIFICATION' of both the press and politics in Nigeria organized around his West African Pilot.

With this newspaper the medium become the message of politics with its goal of immediate and total independence.

It was no accident that almost all the politicians of Southern Nigeria during the First Republic and many of those of the Second Republic were journalists. In the North, since the totality of the elite were working with or for the colonial government, there was only one newspaper, Gaskiya, established by the government in 1939 and censored by both the government and the NA.

Following independence in 1960 the mass media followed the political process in evolving an express tri-polar pattern. This implied a political change from organs protecting the rights of citizens and of Nigeria as a nation, to instrumental organs for the defense of new regional ruling parties. Things did not change much until 1966 when a number of Northern and Western leaders were assassinated in the coup d'état. The result was the media in the North and West became reoriented towards the fight against perceived Igbo domination. The New Nigerian in particular engaged in a campaign which former editor Mamman Daura called the defense of the interests of the Northern elite (Daura 1971).

Press freedom grew in Nigeria in spite of draconian attempts by the state to control it. Even Iwe Irohin was sanctioned by Governor H.S. Freeman for its prejudicial effects on Her Majesty's policies (Concord Weekly 13.5.85). In 1903, the Newspapers Ordinance was passed to control the press and in 1909 a Sedition Ordinance was passed to strengthen the first law.

Journalists such as Herbert Macaulay were imprisoned several times under these laws.

With independence, the anti-press laws were strengthened instead of being liberalized. In 1962 an Official Secrets Act was enacted. Elt was under this law that *Newbreed* and *Newswatch* magazines were proscribed in 1978 and 1987 respectively.[3] The 1903 Ordinance was strengthened with the 1964 Newspapers [Amendment] Act and in 1984 the Public Officers Protection Against False Accusation Decree was enacted to establish finally that 'protection of public servants' rather than 'truth' should be the basic principle of journalism. Although the present regime has abrogated this last decree, their attitude towards the press is even more authoritarian than their predecessors. The then Chief of General Staff Aikhomu warned chief executives of Federal, and state-owned media that they 'will henceforth be held responsible for any adverse stories published by their organs.... It would be an offence for any of their organs to criticize Government policy' (Reporter 11.2.88). Using these laws and often going beyond them, government has imprisoned, detained, tortured, harassed and often sacked numerous journalists for writing things that are unpleasant to the state. Minere Amakiri, for example, was detained and tortured in 1968 by Governor Diete-Spiff's aide de camp for an embarrassing story of the Governor's birthday.

The court, however, granted Amakiri damages. Much more disturbing is the murder of Dele Giwa, a popular Journalist, by a parcel bomb in 1906. This is the first case of murder in the 130-year old history of Nigerian journalism.

In spite of all these problems the Nigerian press remains one of the freest in Africa. The role the press played during the colonial struggle has already been mentioned. During the First Republic we could cite the role the press played to force the government to abrogate the Anglo-Nigerian Defence Pact and force the Prime Minister, Abubakar Tafawa Balewa, to terminate the services of Peter Stallard. Stallard, an English citizen, was Secretary of the Government and Head of Service after Independence.

Military regimes have also suffered from vigorous press campaigns. The Gowon regime lost its credibility following press revelations of corrupt practices by Joseph Tarka, the Commissioner of Communications and Governor Gomwalk of Benue Plateau State. The New Nigerian newspaper in particular seemed to have enjoyed remarkable freedom of expression. At the beginning of the civil war, this newspaper bluntly refused to obey an order from General Gowon to withdraw an embarrassing publication on Col. George Kuruba. They later published a series of articles on 'upstarts, corruption and generals who has not been to the war front', a direct attack on the then Head of State (Ibrahim 1983: 153). This incident is a reminder that in Nigeria the publicly-owned media are often more independent of state control than the private media, even if the competition imposed by the latter obliges the former to improve its journalism.

In spite of the economic crisis that has hit Nigeria since 1981-82, there has been an exceptional growth of magazines and newspapers this decade, a situation that leads to higher quality investigative Journalism. By 1987, Nigeria had 23 dailies, 39 weeklies, 9 vernacular newspapers, 54 magazines, 29 radio stations and 32 television stations (West Africa 16.2.87). Since then many more have sprung up in preparation for the formation of political parties and elections in 1989/90. This huge mass media constitutes a formidable challenge to arbitrary government action. No wonder Group Captain Samson Omeruah, the Minister of Information, complained early in 1988 that the media are characterized by a 'bring down the government syndrome.'

There are two other forms of mass communications that play an important role in the struggle for democracy in Nigeria pamphleteering and literature. Political pamphleteering in Nigeria started as far back as 1908 when Herbert Macaulay distributed 1000 pamphlets documenting mal-administration at the Nigerian Railways and the role of Governor Egerton in 'wicked appropriation of land... personification of prejudice... and scandals.' (Omu 1978: 182). Pamphleteering developed as a complement to the press as it was usually used for sensitive issues that could not easily be printed in newspapers. Macaulay for example printed his pamphlet to side track the 1903 Press Ordinance. Similarly when in 1974 Tai Solarin could not get his stinging article 'The Beginning of the End' published in the press he distributed it as a pamphlet. Solarin warned General Gowon to stick to his earlier promise to hand over power in 1976 or else it would be the beginning of his end. The General refused to, listen and was thrown out of office a few months later. The Nigerian left in particular has, over the past few years, developed pamphleteering into a fine art.

And, finally literature. In his essay on the contribution of Wole Soyinka to the struggle for democracy in Nigeria and in Africa Alain Ricard (1988. 51) had drawn our attention to Alioune Diop's inaugural text in the Presence Africaine series in 1947. Literatures Diop announced, has become an institution like Parliament. Since then parliaments have evolved and disappeared in Africa, but literature has remained "as the voice of public opinion - talking for those who are not military officers, big 'merchants or landlords and who therefore need justice in their country". The works of Chinua Achebe, Cyprian Ekwensi, Wole Soyinka and Festus Lyayi have done more for the struggle to liberalize the politics of Nigeria than the stultified and uninspiring works of political scientists and sociologists.

B. Trade Union Struggles

The dynamism of trades, professional and students unions in Nigeria is one of the clearest signs of the democratic drive embedded in its civil society. The ability of trade unions to carry out their basic functions of struggling to improve the material and social conditions of labor is itself an important aspect of the democratic struggle. In this section, we shall confine ourselves to the political demands in favor of democracy made by unions rather than on trade unionism itself.

The Nigerian nationalist movement took its elan in 1945 following the general strike organized by the unions that year. The general strike was in fact proceeded by a mass campaign "that in the hands of workers and not capitalists lies the freedom of the world". (Coleman, 1986:257) The general strike by crippling the railways, postal and telegraph services among others, virtually paralyzed the colonial system and demonstrated its weakness when confronted with the popular will.

Since then, the trade union movement, in conjunction with progressive movements and organizations have consistently fought for the rights of the common man. The general strikes of June 1964 and May 1981 were organized at critical periods of significant erosion of human and civic rights by the State. The Nigerian State tried to completely destroy trade unionism in 1977-1978 with a purge of "Marxist" leaders. The most prominent radical unionists were banned and a new central labor Organization, the Nigerian Labor Congress (NLC) was established. During the NLC elections, another generation of radical unionists under the leadership of Hassan Sunmonu emerged. In addition, a common front was created between the NLC, the National Association of Nigerian Students (NANS) and the Academic Staff union of Universities (ASUU) to organize popular struggles for improved conditions of life as well as to resist State repression. In 1986 for example, a mass protest movement emerged against the killing of demonstrating students in Zaria while in April another series of demonstration were organized following IMF inspired increase in the price of petrol.

Nigerian students have been playing a very significant role since 1934 when they established the Lagos Youth Movement, the core on which the first nationalist party, the NCNC was built. In the post war years, the West African Students Union played a galvanizing role in the independence movements. The 1959, "march on Lagos' of students of the University of Ibadan, precipitated the press campaign against the "Anglo-Nigerian Defense Pact." Similarly, the spontaneous students demonstrations that followed the assassination of the popular General Murtala Mohammed in February, 1976 which helped in preventing the retrogressive Dimka led coup d'état.

For ASUU, radicalization was a product of the trade union struggles lecturers found themselves involved in to improve their conditions of work, enhance academic freedom and improve the quality of university education. Other professional associations such as the Nigerian Bar Association (NDA) and even the National Association of Resident Doctors and the Nigerian Medical Association have struggled for improved social services. The last President of ASUU correctly noted that the; "1984 - 1988 period seems to be quite remarkable in the sense of the growing concern of professional bodies with the erosion of Nigeria's democratic process, their increasing demands for broad socioeconomic reforms and mounting agitation for the restoration of denied democratic and human rights."(Jega, 1988)

In fact since the NLC's Worker's Charter of Demands in 1980 and NAN's Students Charter of Demands in 1982, there has been a growing consciousness that specific economic and social demands Could be met only if the frontiers of democracy are broadened. From the point of view of the State however, there is a growing "counter-consciousness" that the Nigerian bourgeoisie could only be protected by restricting human rights and tightening the frontiers of democracy. This accounts for the frequent ban orders, termination of appointments, detentions and other repressive measures unions professional organizations and their leaders have been subjected to. Increased repression is further reinforced by the difficulties faced by the Nigerian State in its attempt to impose the IMF inspired structural adjustment program which is strongly resisted by Nigerian civil society.(Ibrahim, 1988:B)

C. The Judicial System

We have already mentioned that law was one of the few respectable professions that was open to educated Africans under the colonial system. Being called to the bar was a ticket not only to a reasonably high income but also to respect in law as well in public esteem. No wander clans and villages taxed themselves to send a "son of the sail' to Britain to study law. The result was that Nigeria produced so many lawyers that their influence went beyond the country's borders into other Anglophone countries[2]

For all these lawyers, most of whom were in private practice, to be able to maintain their elevated place in society, the judicial machine must operate in a fairly just and non arbitrary manner. In other words, the average plaintiff should be convinced that the lawyer could make a difference in solving his problem and is thus ready to Pay. Lawyers therefore had a corporate interest in the maintenance of due process, the rule of law and civil liberties.

The fact that lawyers became a powerful pressure group as well as the technocrats that drafted Nigerian Constitutions and laws played an important role in maintaining this legal culture. In addition, they were able to guide subsequent military regimes to keep to the form even if not to the essence of judicial process.

---

[2] Professor Amlot of the University of London in a lecture at the University of Bordeaux in June 1987 argued that Nigeria jurists were so predominant in the Bench and Bar of Anglophone countries such as Gambia, Tanzania and Zambia that the country could be accused of legal sub-imperialism

Military regimes were for example constrained to enact new decrees that would repeal or bypass existing laws that hinder their objectives rather than act in a "might is right" manner. This legal fetishism often transgresses the course of justice and the spirit of the law but to a certain extent, legalism slow down political arbitrariness especially as until recently, no law or decree in Nigeria has been retroactive.

The principles of the rule of law have however been increasingly threatened by the State in recent years. Decree no.2 of 1984 still in vigor allows the Chief of General Staff to detain citizens' for extended periods without charging them to court.

The decree suspends the important instrument of HABEAS CORPUS that citizens could use to compel the State to produce detainees in court. It should be remembered that in April 1961, the three 'National Government' leaders; Ahmadu Bello, Micheal Okpara and Tafawa Balewa met and decided to enact this type of detention law but resistance to their plans were too strong. (African Concord 16/8/1988, p.16) It has taken the Nigerian State 23 years of effort' to be able to impose this repugnant law.

The Nigerian legal system is however still in a fairly combative mood. In 1984, the whole legal profession rose against the suspension of due process and systematization of military tribunals to 'persecute" rather than 'prosecute" politicians. They are now trying to resist the authoritarian excesses of the Babangida regime. The assassination of Dele Giwa, editor of *Newswatch* magazine for example has led to an important civil liberties case. Dele Giwa was said to have been interrogated arid threatened just before his death by Col. Halilu Akilu the Director of Military Security and Lt. Col. A. K. Togun, Deputy Director of State Security over a lead story he was preparing.

In spite of the suspicious circumstances that surrounded his death, the Director of Public Prosecutions was unwilling to prosecute the two officers and a private lawyer, Gani Fawehinmi decided to take the matter up in court. in a historic judgement delivered on 18th December 1987 the Supreme Court authorized private persons to prosecute criminal cases that have not been taken up by the Public Prosecution Department.

While the numerous substantive cases raised by the judgement are still in court, the Government, pushed to the wall has detained Fawehinmi. In recent years, the struggle by lawyers and other activists for human rights has been assuming a sharper organizational focus. In 1985, an Association of Democratic

Lawyers was formed and in 1987 a Civil Liberties Organization (CLO) emerged to coordinate the struggle for civil liberties. In December 1988, the CLO published a report on Human Rights Violation in Nigeria as a working document to help in the fight against arbitrariness by the State and its agents.

This brief overview of the Nigerian mass medial trades and professional unions and the judicial system reveals clearly that there are a number of democratic assets embedded in the country's civil society. Their force and relevance lies in the relative autonomy they have enjoyed vis-a-vis the State. This autonomy is frequently subjected to serious threats by the State but the capacity for resistance has been significantly high.

III: THE MILITARY: PLAYING CINCINATUS OR IS IT THE SWORD OF DAMOCLES?

Military Regimes in Nigeria have presented themselves as actors playing a role that resembles that of Cincinatus. (Oyovbaire, 1987:178) In Roman mythology, Cincinatus was a legendary hero whom in a period of social decay was called upon to perform the civic duty of rebuilding social norms and institutions to recreate the greatness of the Roman Empire. Having successfully performed his assignment, he scorned the 'glories' of public office and returned to private life.

The Nigerian military it is true have never made claims to perpetual rights to power as is the case in so many other African countries. In 1966, Major General Aguiyi Ironsi, the first military Head of State stated unambiguously in his takeover speech that military intervention would be a brief civic duty 'to maintain law and order in the Federation 'until such a time as a new Constitution for the Federation, prepared in accordance with the wishes of the people is brought into being.' (Kirk-Green 1980:70). Subsequent military takeovers have always claimed allegiance to this principle. The present Head of State, General Babangida has formally declared that 'military rule is an aberration."(West Africa 20/4/1987, p.1897) The Nigerian Military has therefore presented its political interventions as necessary "corrective regimes".

They have in fact performed a number of "corrections" on Nigeria's body politic. First of all, they have transformed the geopolitical base of the country's politics. The tripartite political structure which became quatripartite with the creation of the Mid West in 1963 was profoundly transformed with the creation of 12 states in 1967 increased to 19 states in 1976 and 21 states in 1987, all by military regimes. Thanks to this transformation, the 'minorities" that were politically repressed b., their respective 'majorities during the 1st republic became "liberated'. It was this situation that enabled the minority ethnic groups to become the decisive factor in the 1979 General Elections.(Ollawa, 1981)

Secondly, the military eroded' the power' base of' chiefs (traditional rulers) by dismantling the system of Native Administration(NA). Successive local government reforms led to the withdrawal of judicial, Police and detention powers from the so called traditional authorities thus leaving them with only informal and residual powers. The third heritage of the military is the creation of a strong centralized State structure. The successive multiplication of States has produced clearly discernable Jacobin effect on federal power. Kashim Ibrahim, former Governor of Northern Nigeria put it clearly;

> "Increasing miniaturization of states consequent on creation of puny states has also led to a loss of some of the freedoms inherent in a federal system of government. The system stresses unity and diversity and a powerful federal or central government legally so constituted with a constellation of financially subservient and dependent states... lends itself to dictatorship because there is little or no room for the states to maneuver."(Osuntokun, p.1218)

Nigerian federalism has thus become increasingly unitary with the states having devolved rather than exclusive powers. The decision of the Federal Government in October 1988 to directly fund local governments without going through the states and the consequent abrogation of ministries of local governments in the states is bound to strengthen central vis-a-vis local power. This centralizing heritage created by the military is so strong that it is now generally accepted in ruling class circles that a strong president 'protected" from institutional controls is necessary even civilian regimes. (Ibrahim 1986)

Although the military have significantly political structures and institutions, their impact on political culture is less impressive. Unlike the Roman Cincinatus, Nigerian military "politicians" have not scorned the spoils of office.'

They have learned from their civilian predecessors the "art, of the use of political power for personal enrichment, a process that has profound effects on the evolution of democracy in Nigeria.

IV: Antinomies of Neo-patrimonial Development and Liberal Democracy

Nigerian Politicians and their local friends and allies that Came to power in the 1950s have since then used state Power to enrich themselves (Osoba 1977 and Ibrahim 1987). After over thirty years of pillage from the state and by the states a certain type of bourgeoisie has been created by a development process often described as neo-patrimonial because of the reduction of economies to politics and the equation of power with wealth (Medard 1982).

The principal question that is posed is whether this type of ruling class, whose reproduction as a ruling class is completely dependent on its direct control of state power could tolerate democracy - a political process that threatens and reduces direct political appropriation of wealth. To put it differently, a democratic political process presents a clear problematic to Nigerian political actors. For the rising neo-patrimonial bourgeoisie, democracy is a direct threat to its political means of production' or rather means of appropriating rent'. For the people, democracy is a means of broadening popular participation in the fruits of economic development.

Some studies on the travails of democracy and capitalist development in Indonesia, India and Pakistan give useful comparative indications on the problematic posed. For Indonesia, Tornquist (1988: 44) argues that the domestic bourgeoisie which was very weak 'fought actively for democracy'. It then used the political patronage that parliamentary democracy provided it to strengthen its accumulation through rent. As they grew stronger 'they abandoned even quite limited forms of people's rule and enforced corporatist consensus oriented and authoritarianism rent-interventionist state.' (Tornquist 1988: 141)

For the Indian sub-continent, Martinussen argues the relative strength or weakness of the bourgeoisie was the basic factor determining democratic or autocratic forms of regimes. In the Pakistani part, the national bourgeoisie was relatively weak. In order to secure the promotion of its interests through the' state apparatuses it has been necessary therefore, to establish and maintain a bureaucratic-autocratic form of regime' (Tornquist 1988: 10).

In contrast, in the Indian part of the sub-continent, the national bourgeoisie not only had a dominant economic position but was also well organized on the political scene, including the party political scene and the representative-legislative assemblies. 'Consequently, the Indian bourgeoisie was capable of promoting its interests through the state apparatuses even under a parliamentary--democratic form of government.' (Tornquist 1988: 10) The strength of the bourgeoisie is therefore a very important factor in the constitution of the liberal-autocratic political forms.

The Nigerian situation is significantly different from the Asian one. By the time Nigerians took control of political power, there was no Nigerian bourgeoisie.

There wasn't even a strong merchant class as colonial trading companies and the colonial state had destroyed the pre-colonial trade network and monopolized colonial trade. The politicians that came into power in the 1950s therefore had the historic task of 'fabricating' a bourgeoisie almost uniquely from political resources. The classical Marxist notion of dominant class forces at the level of production structuring the use of state power has to be inverted to understand the nature of Nigerian capitalism and its state. Beckman's (1985) otherwise excellent article on capitalism and the state in Nigeria misses the point by trying to find out whether the Nigerian state is an organ of international capital,' domestic bourgeoisie, or capital in general as if all the three are not themselves products of the State.

All forms of capital gain access to the Nigerian economy through the state and the governing group that controls the state. The State is the instrument of accumulation.

The Nigerian political economy is characterized above all by the primacy of politics and the basis of accumulation is political power (Claude Ake 1985) has correctly argued that this primacy of politics is the major impediment, not only to democratic process, but also to the constitution of the ruling class itself. The acquisition of power is the condition for the accumulation of capital and the loss of power signifies immediate marginalization. With the stakes being so high and so absolute the struggle for power assumes Hobbesian dimensions. During the first Republic, this struggle took the form of regionalism and ethnicity. The parliamentary system became completely blocked because nobody could afford to lose power. The stakes were too high and it needed a civil war to unblock the system. During the Second Republic, regionalism and 'ethnicity were less intense, only to be replaced by a vicious' struggle over religion and over the control of political parties.

The nomination of candidates for electoral posts, in particular through the use of party thugs, money and other means became a major crisis point for all parties. Francis Nzeribe, a top Nigerian capitalist, claims to have invested, yes invested,

$12 million to get a Senate seat, and that part of the money was to pay for the 10, 000 thugs he needed to assure his 'election'. Appearing before the London bankruptcy court, he explained that a coup d'état occurred just three months after his election, so that he could not recover his investment, not to talk of profit (West Africa 23.2.87). No wonder Nzeribe defined democracy as' rigging for rigging, naira for naira, stockfish for stockfish, thuggery for thuggery.

Not surprisingly, the Second Republic ended in a virtually undeclared' civil war. It is this fear that liberal democracy could lead to a Hobbesian war of all against all that is leading the Nigerian ruling to class to demand for a Leviathan in the form of a strong and unchecked President.

At the level of elections, the struggle for power translates into systematic rigging. Justice Ovie Whiskey, Chairman of FEDECO, had described the 1983 elections as 'the freest ever' (Guardian 9.11.95). But two years later, after more serious reflection, he could not but declare that '.Nigeria is not ready for free and fair elections'. (West Africa 9.3.87). The report of experts on the 1983 elections prepared by the National Institute of Policy and Strategic Studies correctly predicated a few months' before the elections that rigging and violence would be the order of the day because 'wealth' had replaced the criterion of 'free and fair competition' (NIPSS 1983: 11). The report pointed out further that no government was ready to accept the' ' ' possibility of losing power and that only the elections of 1959 and those of 1979 had been relatively free and fair - due to the existence of powerful supervisory authorities, the colonial authorities for the former and the military for the latter (NIPSS 1983:.3).

A striking paradox in Nigerian politics is that apart from the undemocratic negation of free choice characteristic of civilian regimes, the civilians also seem to be less concerned about human rights.' ' This is not an indication that the military are' more liberal or democratic. In fact the contrary is the case.

Civilian regimes are obliged to function within a framework of democratic institutions. This means the acts of private appropriation of public resources are more open and thus easily seen and contested by the public. In addition, politicians are open to organized public exposure and scrutiny by opposition parties. It is in relation to this incessant public scrutiny that those in power tend to be more repressive to assure their survival. The great advantage of liberal democracy In countries such as Nigeria is that its relative openness has a didactic effect on the People. Everybody could, on his own demystify politics and state -

that it has nothing to do with 'general interests' but is simply a question of private greed denying 'the people' their wealth by gormandizing everything themselves.

Military regimes in contrast are less sectarian and more corporatist in terms of how they organize the political elite. The absence of sectarian elite conflict results in a more opaque process of appropriating public resources. As the public cannot contest what it does not know, the military and their civilian collaborators steal in a more serene and peaceful atmosphere so they have less necessity of repressing civil liberties that could question the process of accumulation for the simple reason that there is much less public contestation.

The essential problematic for democracy posed by the neo-patrimonial manner in which capitalism is developing in Nigeria is that public resources are increasingly being controlled and used in an undemocratic way. This means that at this time, democracy is a threat to the bourgeoisie because it questions their means of accumulation in addition to amplifying intrabourgeois conflicts and thus threatening the existence of the proverbial goose (the state) that lays the golden egg (the national cake). For the people democracy is an important means of acquiring the intrinsic qualities of civil liberties compelling the state to 'trickle down' public resources and learning the true vices of capitalism and thus Increasing their capacity to combat it (or succumb to it).

V: Towards the Third Republic

The political transition program that is to prepare the way the Third Republic and the new Constitution that has been drafted pose additional dangers for the future of democracy in the country. For the first time in Nigerian history, a Constitution formally limits the number of political parties to be registered and in fact reduces their number to two. We have argued that the tripartite system of the First Republic was exclusionary even though it had no on the number of parties. It however had a little room for maneuver left for sociological and ideological minorities who could legally form parties and struggle to maintain and expand their political space.

It is this possibility that the State has decided to block. By imposing bipartisan system, the multiplicity of groups, forces, ideologies, interests, parties etc that have helped create a democratic culture in Nigeria could be forced Lo coalesce into two political oligarchies. And he who says two oligarchies says one oligarchy for a sole opposition party, excluded from power and subjected to the carrot and stick, tactics of harassment and incorporation might easily be pushed into impotence. To put it differently, General Babangida's transition program could very well be a formula for producing a "sultanic president" or a unified presidential oligarchy that could impose its authoritarianism on the country.

To determine the two political parties to be registered, the National Electoral Commission(NEC) and the government imposed very expensive preconditions that only the upper section of the bourgeoisie could have afforded. In three months, the Parties were to establish well equipped offices with at least three paid staff in all the 435 local government areas in the country. In addition, they here to supply 25 copies of the names, photographs and personal detail is of at least 200 members from each local government (making at least 87,000 files) to the NEC. 13 parties were able to submit their files before the deadline, but in October 1969, the Government announced that none of the parties was sufficiently national in outlook or free of rich sponsors so none of them would be registered. The Government therefore decided that it would itself establish the two parties that would contest, one for right wing citizens and the other for left wing citizens. In other words, it is the State rather than the people that would operate the "democratic and national political parties."

CONCLUSION

Nigeria enjoys one of the most advanced democratic cultures in Africa because of certain specificity's in its historical evolution (see Share 1987:526). There are two aspects. First, the differential growth in space and time of political structures and institutions. The differences in background and interest between strands of the elite were sufficient to block the emergence of a hegemonic bloc that could have turned into an authoritarian oligarchy. There emerged a situation similar to India's (Tornquist, 153) characterized by a 'regulative democracy' to manage, mediate and forge compromise between Progressives and conservatives, ethnic majorities and regions and religions etc. No Leviathan could emerge to impose his "notion of national unity".

The second aspect is that democracy is never given, it is obtained. In this respect, Nigerian civil society has a rich tradition of struggle for civil and human rights. The mass media, trades and professional unions and the judicial system have evolved as bulwarks against State arbitrariness. This democratic drive is however confronted by a strong authoritarian will by succeeding regimes who need repression to maintain their power and the "fruits" it provides. Nigeria's democratic assets are therefore threatened by the neo-patrimonial character of the bourgeoisie's process of accumulation. There is an additional threat posed by the politicization of primary cleavages, especially religion, which threatens not only the evolving democracy but also the State itself.

Finally, the point should be made that the preservation of democracy is not a simple function of assets and problems, it is also a question of historical will. Nigerians have demonstrated a will to preserve hard won democratic rights and if they are trained in the art of provocation, they are also trained in the art of compromise. The country could evolve towards an open regulative democracy based on the rule of law and the preservation of civil liberties rather than a dangerous and rigid consociational "democracy" composed of cabals representing authoritarian oligarchies.

* See Jibo Ibrahim (1992) "The State Accumulation and Democratic forces In Nigeria" in Lars Rudebeck(ed.)(1992) *When Democracy makes sense: Studies In the Democratic Potential of Third World Popular Movements* (Uppsala, Sweden: AKUT).

NOTES

1) Claude Ake, "The Nigerian State: Antinomies of Formation" in C. Ake (ed.) THE POLITICAL ECONOMY OF N SERIAL Longman London, 1985.
2) Yusuf Bangura, "The Crises of Underdevelopment and the Transition to Civil Rule; Conceptualizing the Question of Democracy in Nigeria, Paper for the Nigerian Political Science Association, Ibadan, July, 1988.
3) Bjorn Beckman, "Neo-colonialism, Capitalism and the State in Nigeria" in H. Bernstein and B. Canpbell (eds.) CONTRADICTIONS OF CAPITALISM IN AFRICA, SAGE Publications, Beverly Hills, 1984.
4) Isaac Bora, THE TWELVE DAY REVOLUTION, Idodo Umeh Publishers, Benin City, 1982.
5) James Coleman, NIGERIA: BACKGROUND T0 NATIONALISM reprint by Broburg Wistrom, Benin City, 1986.

6) Mamman Daura, "Editing a Government Newspaper in Nigeria" in 0.Stokke(ed)REPORTING AFRICA, Scandinavian Institute of African Studies, Uppsala, 1971.
7) Taslim Elias (ed) NIGERIAN PRESS LAW, Evans Brothers, London, 1969.
8) Guy Hermet, "Comment naissent les democraties', ESPRIT, no. 6, Juin, 1984.
9) Jibrin Ibrahim, THE POLITICAL ECONOMY OF MASS COMMINICATIONS IN NIGERIA, M. Sc. thesis, ABU, Zaria, 1983.
10) "The Political Debate and the Struggle for Democracy in Nigeria" ROAPE, no. 37, 1986.
11) 'De l'acquisition primitive du pouvoir a l'acquisition du capital" DEA, Bordeaux, i987.
12) "Les uniformes des lyceennes nigriannes" POLITIQUE AFRICAINE, no. 29, mars, 1988.
13) "La societe (nigerianne) contre le bipartisme" Politique Africaine, no. 32, decembre 1988.
14) "Politics and Religion in Nigeria. - The Parametre of the 1987 Crisis in Kaduna States' ROAPE,
15) and Ibrahim Muazzam 'Some Comments on Babangida's Transition Program" Paper for Nigerian Political Science Association Conference, lbadan, July, 1988.
16) Attahiru Jegal "The Relevance of Authorized Professional Groups Under Military Rule: The Nigerian Experience" Paper for Nigerian Bar Association Conferences Kaduna September 1988.
17) Richard Joseph, Democracy and Prebendal Politics in Nigeria: The Rise and Fall of the Second Republic. Cambridge University Press, 1987.
18) Anthony Kirk-Green, Stay By Your Radio, AfrikaStudrecentrum, Linden, 1980.
19) A. M Mainasara, The Five Majors: Why They Struck, Hudahuda, aria, 1982.
20) John Martinussen, Social Classes And Forms Of State And Regimes In Peripheral Societies, AKUT no. 24, Uppsala, 1982.
21) Jean-Francois Medard, "The Underdeveloped State in Tropical Africa: Political Clientelism or Neo-Patrimonialism" in C. Clapham(ed) Private Patronage And Private Power, France-Pinter, London, 1982.
22) Jean-Francois Medard "De la democratic en Afrique: quelques observations", Bordeaux, mimeo, 1987.

23) D. J. M. Muffet, *Let Truth Be Told, The Coups D'etat Of 1966*, Hudahuda, Zaria, 1982.
24) New Horizons *"NLC - NANS - ASUU Front"*, July 1986.
25) New Horizon, *"NLC Has Widened Its Popular Struggle"* March, 1908.
26) Guy Nicholas, "Les Nations a polarisations variable et leur Etat:le cas Nigerian, in E. Terray, (ed) L'ETAT CONTEMPORAIN EN AFRIQUE, Harmattan, Paris, 1987.
27) NIPSS, *"Round - Table Meeting on the 1983 General Elections"*, Kuru, 1983.
28) Patrick Ollawa, "The Nigerian Elections of 1979: A Further Comment", *Journal of Commonwealth and Comparative Politics*, vol. nXIX, no. 3, November 1981.
29) Fred Omu, *PRESS AND POLITICS IN NIGERIA: 1880 - 1937* Longman, lbadan 1978.
30) Segun Osoba, "The Nigerian Power Elite. 1952-1965' in P. Gutkind and P. Waterman, *African Social Studies: A Radical Reader*, Heineman, London, 1977.
31) A. Osuntokun, *Power Broker: A Biography Of Sir Kashim Ibrahim*, Spectrum, lbadan, 1987.
32) Samson Oyovbaire, "The Context of Democracy in Nigeria' and "Democratisation and the Political Process. The Sward of Damocles" in S. E. Oyovbaire (ed) *Democratic Experiment In Nigeria:Intepretive Essays,* Omega Publishers, Benin City, 1987.
33) Alain Ricard, *Wole Soyinika Ou L'ambition Democratique*, Les nouvelles editions africaines, Paris, 1988.
34) Donald Shares "Transition to Democracy and Transition through Transaction" *Comparative Political Studies*, vol. 19.

Chapter Two

Grassroot Mobilization and Constitutional Development in Nigeria (1960-1992)

Sylvester O. Fajoyomi*

Each time the army seizes power in Nigeria, the scenario is always the same. After blaming the politicians for non - respect of the Constitution, the Constitution itself is accused of inadequacies. Effectively, a group of people, intellectuals, politicians and businessmen are brought together with a view to reviewing the said Constitution and to drafting a new one that will serve the country after the withdrawal of the military. So it was during Major General Ironsi's regime (Nigeria' first military regime).[1] Gowon's regime that followed *was* no exception.[2] It was Murtala Mohammed *cum* Obasanjo government that finally accelerated the efforts which led to the birth of the Constitution of the Second Republic.[3] The fall of that Republic in December 1983 has made the a repeat of the scenario possible. The military government of General Babangida took the same steps to give a new Constitution to Nigeria. From the Political Bureau to the Constitution Review Committee (CRC) and to the Constituent Assembly (CA), the government adopted a new Constitution for the Third Republic on the 3rd of May 1989.[4]

Is this Constitution different from the previous one? If yes, how far? Is it capable of taking care of the inadequacies of which the previous one was accused of? How far can the Constitution guarantee the stability of the Third Republic? These are some of the questions this article will try to answer.

---

* Paper presented at the AKUT Conference on "When Does Democracy Make Sense", at the University of Uppsala. (October 26-28, 1989)

BACKGROUND TO THE CONSTITUTION

In his maiden broadcast[5] after the military coup of December 31 1983, the Head of State, Major General Buhari did not make mention of his government's commitment to return the country to civil rule. On the other hand, he addressed the issues[6] that brought the military back to power after four years of civilian government. He said : "The last Federal military Government drew up a program with the aim of handling over political power to the civilians in 1979. That program as you know was implemented to the letter.

The 1979 Constitution was promulgated. However, little did the military realize that the political leadership of the Second Republic would circumvent most of the checks and balances in the Constitution and bring us to the present stage of general insecurity. The premium on political power became exceedingly high that political contestants regarded victory at the elections as a matter of life and death struggles and were determined to capture or retain power by all means".[7] He then went ahead to list the priority program of his government. The Federal Military Government he said, "will reappraise policies with a view to paying greater attention to the following areas

a) The economy will be giving a new impetus and better sense of direction.

b) Corrupt officials and their agents will be brought to book.

c) In view of the droughts that affected most parts of the country the Federal Military Government will, within the available resources, import foodstuff to supplement the shortfalls suffered in the last harvest.

d) Payment of salary arrears to workers.

e) Our foreign policy will both be dynamic and realistic. Africa will, of course, continue to be the center-piece of our foreign policy.

f) The morale and combat readiness of the Armed Forces will be given high priority. Officers and men with high personal and professional integrity will have nothing to fear"[8]

This showed indications that the Buhari government, up till the time it was overthrown in August 1985, was really not ready to set in motion the machine that would have returned the country to civil democratic government. The approach of the Babangida administration was quite different. Right from the time he assumed power, President Babangida laid down the forum for discussion, debates and consultations to try once again and construct a new political order in Nigeria.

It is in this context that the President in the Budget Speech of January 1, 1986 announced the establishment of a Political Bureau. He said: "in order to establish a viable and enduring people-oriented political system, devoid of perennial disruptions, this Administration has decided to involve the people in the search for a solution to the problem of political instability which characterized our past democracy in Nigeria".[9]

At its inauguration on the 13 of January, two weeks after it was announced, the President declared, "Today we commence the search for a new political order. I believe the time is now ripe for us to have a system which can guarantee an acceptable and painless succession mechanism".[10]

The 17 -member Political Bureau was then given the mandate to:[11]

a) Review Nigeria's political history and identify the basic problems which have led to our failure in the past and suggest ways of resolving and coping with these problems;

b) Identify a basic philosophy government which will determine goals and serve as a guide to the activities of Government;

c) Collect relevant information and data for the Government as well as identify other political problems that may arise from the debate;

d) Gather, collate and evaluate the contributions of Nigerians to the search for a viable political future and provide guidelines for the attainment of consensus objectives;

e) Deliberate on other political problems as may be referred to it from time to time. The bureau, after considering a number a of factors, decided to operate as follows:[12]

i). stimulating, coordinating and guiding the national political debate through

a. organizing grassroots participation and mobilising the broad masses of the people in the quest for anew political order;

b. encouraging the contributions of professional, academic, economic and social groups and Organization; and

c. seeking the views of men of experience in public affairs;

ii). Collecting all relevant data for the work of the Bureau and for possible use by the government;
iii). Collating, analysing and summarizing the views expressed in the course of the national political debate;
iv). Review Nigeria's political history and identify the basic problems therein and making recommendations for resolving and coping with these problems;
v). Working out a basic philosophy of government for Nigeria;
vi). Preparing a blue print for a future political model or models for the country;
vii). providing a blue print for an economic model consistent with the political order;
viii). providing guidelines for the implementation of the recommended model;
ix).providing a time-sequence for political transition by 1990; and
x). deliberating on any other political matters that may be referred to the Bureau by the Government.

The nationwide debate that followed was guided by comprehensive guidelines prepared by the Bureau which touched issues such as:[13] a philosophy of government for the future, a viable, popular and genuinely democratic political system, human rights, the link between economic and politics in Nigeria, the local government system, traditional rulership and administration, the Armed Forces in Nigerian politics, state and religion, formation of Nigerian political parties, creation of states, national population census, ethnicity in Nigerian politics, and the judiciary and the administration of justice.

There is no doubt that the debate was a success. The Bureau made it possible for all concerned citizens to participate. These included various professional, social and cultural groups in the country. At the end of the debate, the Bureau received a total of over 27,000 contributions excluding many public hearings which took place at State capitals and symposia organized by various unions in the country.

The Political Bureau, after a thorough analysis of Nigeria's political history and the previous problems of democracy in Nigeria came out with its recommendations which could be summarized as follows:

Firstly, a system of socialism in which the State shall be committed to the nationalization and socialization of the commanding heights of the national economy.

Secondly, a presidential system of constitutional democracy together with the corresponding democratic structures and institutions.

Lastly, the Bureau recommended a set of political processes intended to assist the emergence of new social conduct and behavior patterns.

The only area where the government distanced itself from the Bureau was on the issue of socialism. The government accepted the recommendations on the presidential system of government as entrenched in the 1979 Constitution as well as those on the emergence of new social conduct and behavior patterns which include: the re - definition of Nigerian citizenship, the need for continuous social and political mobilization and the banning of certain political and public office holders from participating in politics.

The next stage towards the making of the Constitution of the Third Republic was the inauguration of the 46-member Constitution Review Committee (CRC) in September 1987. Unlike its predecessor, the Constitution Drafting Committee (CDC) of 1975 that was charged with the drafting of the 1979 Constitution, the CRC was only given the mandate to review the report of the Political Bureau. In a word, it was the report of the Bureau and the 1979 Constitution that formed the basis of Nigeria's new constitution.

At the inauguration of the CRC, a lot of questions were raised as regards what it was going to do. There was a need for such interrogations since the Federal Military Government had earlier on adopted a certain number of recommendations made by the Political Bureau.(The two-party system for example.) The chairman of the CRC however felt the committee still had a lot to do and that his committee might come out with constitutional provisions different from the perceptions of the Bureau. He declared: "Our task is to produce a constitution and not to make recommendations...we shall therefore consider all issues we feel should be in a constitution, irrespective of what the Political Bureau has come out with".[14]

The President, one can say, found it difficult to give the committee a free hand for fear of diversion from the already adopted recommendations of the Bureau. This is evidenced in certain declarations made by General Babangida. Defending the two party system for example, he told the members of the CRC that his administration chose the two-party system so as to avoid the past experience of "multiplicity of political parties built around parties anointed by some ethnic groups."[15] To allay the fear of Nigerians that his government was trying to impose its opinion on the committee, the President added, "though you will have materials to guide, nothing precludes you from a fresh consideration of certain major issues which will arise in the course of your deliberations."[16] He then requested that the committee should review the national commitment to "Fundamental Objectives and Directive Principles of the State" which was included in the 1979 Constitution. To the President, the new Constitution should differ from the previous one in being "acceptable, workable, adaptable, enduring and suited to our peculiar circumstances, needs and temperament as a people now and in the foreseeable future."[17]

The Constituent Assembly which considered the report of the CRC was inaugurated May 11, 1988. It consisted of 567 elected and nominated members under the chairmanship *of Anthony Aniogolu,* a retired *supreme court justice.* In his inauguration speech, President Babangida read out a long list of certain issues which he considered as settled: "I should state categorically that the assembly should not indulge itself in the fruitless exercises of trying to alter the agreed ingredients of Nigeria's political order such as federalism, presidentialism, the non-adoption of any religion as a state religion, and the respect and observance of fundamental human rights..."[18] The President also insisted that the two-party system approved by the government and the ban on some former public office holders from seeking elective or public offices must be so recognized by the assembly.

Taking into considerations all the no go areas enumerated by the President, the question one should ask is clear. Is the Constituent Assembly really independent of the military? Would the new Constitution not represent the wishes and the established preference of the military as against those of the people? The President of the CA was of the opinion that the Constitution represents the wishes of all segments of the country. He even explained why:" A Constitution arrived at after such elaborate countrywide consultations with the people, coupled with the fact that members of the Constituent Assembly represent the opinion of all segments of this country, impels one to confidently say that this is the constitution of the people".[19]

But according to Nwabueze, "a constitution is an act of the people if it is made by them either directly in a referendum or through a convention or a constituent assembly popularly elected for this specific purpose, subject or not to formal ratification by the people in a referendum."[20] In the light of this definition, there is much argument on whether the new Constitution is an act of the people or an act of the Federal Military Government. Firstly, the Constitution was not adopted in a referendum. Secondly, the Constituent Assembly had one-third of its members nominated by the military government.(Among the nominated members were the president, the vice-president and the secretary of the assembly.) Finally, the *378* elected members were elected, not directly by the people but by the local government councilors elected in December 1987. One may be led after considering the arguments above, to say that a constituent assembly elected in this manner could not claim to represent the people, talk less of adopting a constitution on their behalf.

The CA had its ups and downs. The Assembly sat for ten months. The sittings were bedeviled by two major problems which shook the assembly seriously. First was the issue of the Sharia. Committee 16 of the assembly which was given the task to examine the provision for Islamic law could not reach an agreement on what the issue should be in the new Constitution. The Muslims on the committee wanted the sharia extended to the federal level, whereas the Christians felt allowing that will mean that Nigeria is no longer a secular state. At the end of it all, the issue of sharia *was left* as it was in the 1979 Constitution after the military government called the members to order.[21] It is worth mentioning that the same thing happened during the making Of the 1979 Constitution. Then, some members of the assembly staged a walk-out.

Another problem faced by the assembly was that of truancy. The quorum for the conduct of the business of the assembly had to be cut down to 200 from 300 when it was becoming more and more difficult to get the required quorum. What this means is that majority of the members were not even present to debate certain important issues.[22]

THE CONSTITUTION OF 1989 : WHAT'S NEW

The Constitution, for the most part, retained the provisions of its predecessor. The presidential form of government was retained. As pointed out above, the President had earlier on warned the CA not to bother about certain subjects, presidentialism included.

Just like in the 1979 Constitution[23], the President of the Federation is the head of state, the chief executive and commander-in-chief of the Nigerian Armed Forces. He shall hold office for a period of four years renewable for another four only. The motion by the CA to put the tenure of office of the president to a six-year one term was not retained by the government. Those who wanted the change argued that the six years would be enough to have realized any project designed by the executive.

Moreover, the fact that the incumbent would not be seeking re-election would limit rigging and prevent public officers from looting to finance election campaigns. But can't the incumbent finance his party's campaigns? Under the previous constitution, the president had no power to deploy any member of the armed forces of Nigeria on combat duty outside the country without the prior approval of the senate.[24] But in the Constitution, the president is allowed in consultation with the National Defense Council to deploy the army on a limited combat duty outside the country, if he is satisfied that the national security is under imminent threat or danger. But in that wise, the president has to obtain the consent of the senate within seven days of actual combat engagement.[25]

The qualifications for the post of the president did act differ from those enumerated in the 1979 Constitution except that in 1979, a candidate, where there are two shall be deemed to have been duly elected when, firstly, he has majority of the votes cast at the election and secondly, he has not less than one-quarter of the votes cast at the election in each of at least two-thirds of all the states of the federation.[26] The 1989 Constitution retained the first condition of having the majority of votes cast at the election, but changed the second condition to "when he has not less than one-third of the votes cast at the election in each of at least two-thirds of all the states of the federation".[27]

Another novelty is the educational requirement for the future president. The candidate for the presidency shall not be qualified for election if he has not been educated up to at least the school certificate level or its equivalent.[28]

The president appoints the members of the federal executive councils, but unlike in the 1979 Constitution, he no longer needs the confirmation of the senate. While section 141 (i) of the 1979 Constitution states that, " Except in the case of the ex officio members or where other provisions are made in this Constitution, the chairman and members of any of the bodies so established shall, subject to the provisions this Constitution, be appointed by the president, and the appointment

Constitution simply says, all chairmen and members of the bodies so established shall be appointed by the President."

The fact that the senate no longer have a say in the appointment of chairmen and members of such bodies gives the President a blank check to compensate his party men. We do not have instances of problems between the senate and the president during the Second Republic in the appointment of members of such bodies to have warranted the eradication of the confirmatory role of the senate.

Further, under the new Constitution, five new bodies are added to the nine created by the 1979 Constitution. These include: Code of Conduct Bureau; National Boundaries Commission; National Primary Education Commission; Revenue Mobilization Allocation and Fiscal Commission; Public Complaints Commission.[29] In addition, the new Constitution guarantees the freedom of action of some of these bodies, such as the Code of Conduct Bureau, the Federal Civil Service Commission, the Revenue Mobilization, Allocation and Fiscal Commission, the Federal Judicial Service Commission, the National Electoral Commission, the Public Complaints Commission and the National Population Commission.[30]

The importance of the Code of Conduct Bureau under the new Constitution demands a little emphasis. One major problem faced by the Second Republic was corruption. The Code of Conduct Bureau and its Tribunal set up to fight it were not effective. This was because the operation of the Bureau and the Tribunal required an enabling act of the National Assembly. (1979 Constitution 5th Schedule, Part 1.) But during the Second Republic, **no** such law was passed. Under the new Constitution, the Bureau and Tribunal are included in the list of Federal Executive Bodies. This means they are no longer created by an act of the Assembly and as such the Bureau is no longer responsible to the Nation Assembly.

Moreover, under the new Constitution, public officers are supposed to make a declaration of their assets before taking up their appointments and not after as it was under the 1979 Constitution. The experience from the 1979 style was that after taking up offices, government officers refused to declare their assets. As such, "no one was removed from office by the tribunal, and two years after the return to civilian rule, only three people had declared their *assets,* where about two million should have done so under the terms of the code".[31] In implementing that aspect of the Constitution, the Code of Conduct Bureau and its Tribunal have been created by the decree of the military government. The Bureau has offices in each State of the Federation and it *has* started taking declarations of assets from public officers.

The senate still has a say in the appointment of the Auditor-General for the Federation. The candidate has to be, first, recommended by the Federal Civil Service Commission, second, accepted by the president and finally confirmed by the senate.

The confirmatory role that the senate has over the appointment of the Auditor-General takes us to the provisions for the legislature under the new Constitution. Just like its predecessor, the Constitution provides for a bicameral National Assembly : the Senate and the House of Representatives.[32] The National Assembly is vested, by the Constitution, with the legislative power on any matter included in the Exclusive Legislative and in the Concurrent Legislative List.(The two lists are set out in Part 1 and Part II of the Second Schedule respectively.)

Unlike in the 1979 Constitution, [33] the Senate consists of three members from each State and one from the Federal Capital Territory, Abuja. The House of Representatives consists of 453 members, thus having three more than it had in 1979. While the age qualification remains at thirty for the senators, the members of the House of Representatives have to be twenty-five years old.(It was twenty-one years in the 1979 Constitution.)

One novelty in the qualifications for membership of the National Assembly is the provision on education.[34]

Henceforth, to qualify for election as a member of the Assembly, the person must have been educated up to at least School Certificate level or " its equivalent".[35] This new provision is judged necessary if one look back at the proceedings of the Assembly during the Second Republic. It was then rampant to see members sleeping during sessions because they couldn't follow certain debates in English. There were even many of them who couldn't read the Constitution not to talk of being able to figure out what it says on certain issues.

A Constitutional backing was also given to the ban for life of any corrupt or dishonest public officer from seeking elective posts. Whereas the 1979 Constitution limited such ban to ten years before the date of an election to a legislative house, the new Constitution did not state the number of years: "No person shall be qualified for elections to the Senate or the House of Representatives if :...he has been convicted and sentenced by a court of law or tribunal established by law for an offence involving dishonesty or he has been found guilty of a contravention of the Code of Conduct.[36]

This provision, simply interpreted, means that any person found guilty of embezzlement of public fund, as were found most of the politicians of the Second Republic will never again be qualified to stand for election as a member of any legislative house. This might limit corruption not only among politicians but also among future political aspirants.

The procedure for passing a bill into law remains the same as in the 1979 Constitution. A bill may originate in either House. When it has been passed in the House in which it originated, it has to be passed too in the other house and has to be presented to the president for assent before it can become law. If the president does not give his assent and the bill is again passed by each House by two-thirds majority, it becomes law.

There is no change whatsoever in the operation of the judiciary after *the* sharia issue *was* buried. The motion passed by the CRC and the CA to make the judiciary more independent of the executive was not retained by the military government.

Section 78 (6) of the 1979 Constitution states that "the recurrent expenditure of judicial offices of the federation (in addition to salaries and allowances of the judicial officers mentioned in subsection (4) of this section) shall be a charge upon the Consolidated Revenue Fund of the Federation."

The CA in other to make the judiciary totally independent, financially, of the executive and be totally self accounting had recommended that " all moneys, capital and recurrent expenditure due and payable under an appropriation act for the judicial services of the federation, shall be paid into a separate account to be maintained in a bank in Nigeria, and shall be under the control and at the disposition of the Federal Judicial Service Commission"[37] Of interest are certain additions made to the " Fundamental Objectives and Directive Principles of State Policy ". The President specifically requested the CRC to review these objectives. Effectively, to the Political Objectives was added, " the State shall protect and defend the liberty of the individual, enforce the rule of Law and ensure the efficient functioning of governmental services (sec. 16(6)). The new Constitution also allows the State under the Economic Objectives to harness the resources of the nation and promote national prosperity and an efficient, dynamic and self-reliant economy (sec. 17(1)(a)).

The Foreign Policy Objectives too has taken another dimension. In the 1979 Constitution, African unity and eradication of racial discrimination formed the center piece of the country's objectives. Henceforth, the Foreign Policy Objectives include the promotion and protection of the national interest, respect for international law and treaty obligations as well as seeking of settlement of international disputes by negotiation, mediation, conciliation, arbitration and adjudication, and the promotion of a just world economic order (sec. 20).

Another innovation under " Fundamental Objectives and Directive Principles of State Policy" concerns the duties of the citizen. The 1979 Constitution did not have such a provision. The duties of a citizen include, among others, to abide by the Constitution, protect and preserve public property, fight against misappropriation and squandering of public funds, respect the dignity and religion of other citizens. It is also the duty of every citizen to participate in and defend all democratic processes and practices, to declare his income honestly to appropriate and lawful agencies and to pay his tax promptly (sec.24).

The provisions regulating the activities of political parties remain unchanged with the exception of the institutionalization of only two political parties. Thus, section 220(l) of the new Constitution states, "there shall be only two political parties in the federation". The idea of a two-party system was part of the recommendations made by the Political Bureau. When the government lifted the ban on political activities, a number of associations sprang up with intentions to registered as political parties. Most of these associations, according to the government, did not meet the expected requirements for registration.

As such, President Babangida on October 7 1989 came out with a radical solution. He declared, "the AFRC [38] has come to the conclusion that our political problems require radical solutions... To jolt the system a bit".[39] The solution to the problems, according to him, is "a mass platform for the emergence of new Leadership, de-emphasize the role of money in politics and preclude the emergence of political alliances along the lines as in the first and second republics".[40] The government then went ahead to create two parties for the people to join. These are the National Republican Convention (NRC' and the Social Democratic Party (SDP). As the manifestoes of the disbanded associations had their roots in different ideologies, the government directed the National Electoral Commission (NEC) to fashion out constitutions and manifestoes for the two parties with "one a little to the left of the center and the other a little to the right".

The number of parties to contest elections was not specified in the 1979 Constitution.[41]

In the new Constitution, as in the old, the NEC, just like its predecessor, the Federal Electoral Commission (FEDECO), has the right to monitor the accounts of political parties. Of importance is section 226(e) of the 1989 Constitution which states that the National Assembly may by law provide for the maximum amount which any individual is allowed to contribute to a political party. The role of individual money bags was predominant during the Second Republic. This has been reduced to the minimum since the two existing parties are created by the Federal Military Government.

The Local Government system too has been transformed with the provisions of the new Constitution.[42] Henceforth, local governments are considered as the third tier of government. Section 7 of the Constitution not only guarantees its existence just like the previous one did, it also limits the number of Local Governments Areas to 449. This means that any attempt to increase their number will entail an amendment of that section of the Constitution. This provision will evidently prevent a repeat of what happened during the Second Republic, when State governors created new local governments for their own selfish political reasons without adequately taking into consideration their economic viability.

To control corruption, at the local level, the post of the Auditor-General of the Local Governments is created in each State with the duty to audit annually, the accounts of the local governments and thereafter present its report before the State House of Assembly.

Perhaps the most interesting provisions as regards the local government system are those under chapter VIII of the 1989 Constitution. The chapter stipulates how chairmen, vice-chairmen and councilors are to be elected. It also gives guidelines on how to impeach the Chairmen (just like the President and Governors) and how to recall an elected councilor. The Chairman or his vice may be removed from office, according to the new Constitution, when not less than one half of the members of the council found him guilty of gross misconduct in process of performing his functions as the chairman.[43]

This provision may check the dictatorial tendencies of certain chairmen. There is the likelihood that the clause may be abused by the opposition for political gains since the definition of "gross misconduct" is wide.[44] A member of a local government council may be recalled if more than one half of the registered voters in his constituency signed a written petition to the NEC, showing their loss of confidence in him or her.[45] These provisions are likely to instill political awareness at the grassroots.

Local government officials also benefit from the new dispositions. Their rights have been finally entrenched in the Constitution. In order to upgrade their level to that of the State civil service, the Constitution provides for a local government service which guaranties the right of a person in the service of a Local Government to receive pension or gratuity. To effect this is created in each State an executive body, the Local Government Service Commission. The functions of the commission range from setting general guidelines for appointment, promotion and discipline in the Local Government Service to monitoring the activities of each Local Government.[46] One other novelty in the new Constitution is the provision for the establishment of a Traditional Council for a Local Government Area or a group of Local Government Areas.

This is an institutionalization of the advisory role accorded to traditional rulers in the Guidelines for Local Government Reforms of 1976. As from now on, the House of Assembly of the State has the power to create such a council according to the peculiarities of the State. It needs to be stated that the council has no executive, legislative nor judicial powers.[47]

The provision relating to the status of Abuja was also ameliorated. The 1979 Constitution referred to the Federal Capital Territory as if it were one of the States of the Federation. In which case anybody from outside the FCT could be considered as a foreigner. The new Constitution, guarantee the rights of every Nigerian in the FCT. It says "the following special provisions... shall apply to the Federal Capital Territory, Abuja."[48] The FCT will be represented in the National Assembly by a senator and four members in the House of Representatives. The Territory will be constituted into a Mayoralty, with four Area Councils, whose administrative and political structure will be determined by an act of the National Assembly.[49]

As regards the provision concerning religion, fundamental rights and procedure for the creation of more States, nothing was changed. The CA, had initially recommended a modification in the section pertaining to religion to read, "No government shall overtly or covertly give preferential treatment to any particular religion". The government preferred to retain the clause as it was previously entrenched in the 1979 Constitution.

Another decision of the CA not retained by the government is the penalty for coup makers. The CA had put in section 1(4) of the Draft Constitution that "any take-over or control of the government of Nigeria a by any person or persons other than in accordance with the provisions of the present constitution shall remain a punishable crime at all times under Nigerian law".

The reason why the clause was excluded by the military is not clear. The Constitution of the Federal Republic of Nigeria (Promulgation) 1989, marks the beginning of the country's march towards the Third Republic. The need to eradicate corruption and ensure that public servants no longer abuse their offices to amass personal wealth made the Constitution to emphasize the role of the Code of Conduct Bureau and that of its Tribunal. To avoid the excesses of political parties, only two were allowed by the Constitution. The role of the NEC is strengthened so as to check the activities of political parties. A good democratic system must have a well established local government system. Local governments will now be run like other levels of government. Can all these guarantee the stability of the Third Republic?

The stability of the Third Republic can not be judged by the provisions of its constitution. As rightly said Nwabueze, "democracy does not consist mainly of constitutional prescriptions about government and limitations on its power. It is constituted more by national habits, traditions and conventions which condition the attitudes of both the rulers and the governed within a polity, and therefore delimit the parameters of permissible political behavior. It is this --the creation of a national ethic, more than the formal specifications of the Constitution with its nicely balanced structures and powers-- - that determines its success or failure".[50]

The 1989 Constitution, like its predecessor, is a document beautifully construed and based on the works of the Political Bureau, the CRC and the CA. The problem is that the Constitution is going to be operated by individuals who can always translate it to suit their purposes. This is also the view of the chairman of the CA that produced the 1979 Constitution. He said: "The 1979 Constitution took cognizance of the peculiarities of Nigeria. There was nothing wrong with that Constitution. It doesn't matter what constitution you operate, if the people don't want to enforce it you can't do anything".[51] The evils that befell the Second Republic could as well befall the Third. All the shortcomings of the 1979 Constitution could also be found in the 1989 Constitution unless the people are really ready to cooperate and make a success of it. The success or failure of the Constitution depends on the willingness of those concerned to abide by its principles. It is they who detain the key to the stability of the Third Republic.

Note: since this piece was written, the transition program of Babangida led to the election of June 12, 1993 which was almost won by M.K.O Abiola, the result of which was annulled by Babangida and followed by his transferring power to technocrat Sonekan who was later ousted by Sanni Abacha, who in his own turn instituted another transition program that would hand over power to a civilian administration this fall (1998).

NOTES

1) The Head of State of Nigeria's first military government, Major-General Aguyi Ironsi announced on the 21st of February 1966 that he would constitute study groups to review the Constitution of the First Republic (West Africa, 5 March, 1966, P. 279).
2) Gowon initiated an Ad Hoc Conference Constitutional Proposals for Nigeria to reconsider the recommendations of the Study Groups, which led to riots in several parts of the North on 29 and 30 May, 1966
3) For details of how the Constitution was made, see E. Alex Gboyega, "The making of the Nigerian Constitution" in Oyeleye Oyediran (Ed.)'Nigerian Government " Politics under Military Rule 1966-79, The Macmillan Press Ltd, 1979 pp 235-58.
4) Constitution of the Federal Republic of Nigeria (Promulgation) Decree 1989. Decree No. 12
5) First radio and television broadcast of Major General Muhammed Buhari at 20 hours, January 1, 1984. Cited in S.G. Ikoku, Nigeria's Fourth Coup D'état, Options for Modern Statehood. Enugu, Fourth Dimension Publication, 1985.App. IV.
6) Among the issues addressed are shortage of food, corruption, the situation of the country's economy. First radio and television broadcast) op. cit. P. 168
8) Ibid. p.170
9) Budget Speech, The Guardian, 1 January, 1986.
10) See the speech delivered by President Babangida at the inaugural ceremony of the Political Bureau on the 13th of January 1986, attached as Appendix I to the report of the Political Bureau.
11) Ibid.

12) See Federal Government of Nigeria (1987) Government Views and Comments on the Findings and Recommendations of the Political Bureau, Lagos.
13) We have only selected a few issue areas out of the thirty touched by the Bureau.
14) West Africa, 19 October 1987, P. 2067
15) Ibid.
16) Ibid.
17) Ibid. p. 2068
18) Newswatch, March 27 1989, P. 11
19) Ibid. P. 15
20) B. O. Nwabueze, The Presidential Constitution of Nigeria, C. Hurst & Company, London, 1982, P. 1
21. For more on Sharia controversy, see West Africa, November 21-27, 1988, Editorial.
22) Newswatch, op. cit. P. 20
23) The Constitution of the Federal Republic of Nigeria (Enactment)Decree 1978 (Decree No. 25 1978) Chapter VI Part 1.
24) Ibid. Section 5(3)(b)
25) The 1989 Constitution, op. cit. section 5
26) The Constitution 1979 op. cit. sec. 126(l)
27) In a situation where a candidate does not win under the provisions of this section, the National and State Assemblies shall be constituted into an electoral college, by the NEC, to elect the President by a simple majority vote. See section 132(l)(a), (2) and (3).
28) The 1989 Constitution op. cit. sec. 136(l)(a)
29) Ibid. sec. 151
30) The composition and powers of each body are listed in Part 1 of the 3rd schedule of the 1989 Constitution.
31) West Africa, 24 - 30 July, 1989, P. 1203
32) The 1989 Constitution op. cit. chapter V Part 1
33) The 1979 Constitution made provision for five senators from each State of the Federation and one from the Federal Capital Territory.
34) The 1989 Constitution op. cit. sec. 63(2).
35) "Its equivalent" in this section provides for those who might have had Islamic education.

36) The 1989 Constitution op. cit. sec. 64(l)(d).
37) Clause 83 of the Draft Constitution.
38) AFRC means Armed Forces Revolutionary Council.
39) West Africa, 17-23 December 1990
40) Ibid
41) sections 202 to 209 of the 1979 Constitution.
42) Most certain restrictions were listed for these formations; these include their being nationally accepted, that they hold periodic elections to select their leaders which must reflect the federal character of Nigeria, that they must have their headquarters in the Federal Capital Territory etc. For more see of the new provisions for Local Government system under the new Constitution are from the recommendations of two committees: The Dasuki Committee and the Technical Committee on the Implementation of the new Civil Service Reform at the Local Government level.
43) The 1989 Constitution, op. cit. sec. 292
44) Gross misconduct according to the Constitution means " a grave violation of the Oath of Office or grave breach of the provisions of this Constitution or a misconduct of such nature as amounts in the opinion of the Local Government Council to gross misconduct".
45) For the process of recall, see section 304 of the 1989 Constitution.
46) For more on the Local Government Service Commission, see sections 308, 309, 310 and the Third Schedule, Part II D
47) The 1989 Constitution op. cit. sec. 8
48) Ibid. chapter IX et sec. 313
49) Ibid. sec. 315
50) Nwabueze B. O. op. cit. P. vi
51) *Newswatch*, March 27, 1989 P. 15

Chapter Three

The Politics of Political Transition and Military Disengagement 1992-1996

Bamidele A. Ojo

For the fourth time since independence the Nigerian military is engaged in the process of disengaging from politics and hopefully preoccupy itself with its primary role of maintaining and protecting the territorial integrity of the Country. When the first coup occurred in January 1966, the people applauded but in the past five years, the euphoria has disappeared as military rule becomes more and more undesirable. The puritanist, nationalist and the anti-corrupt nature of the military has been eroded by the decadent nature of its administrative practices since its very first involvement.

The Gowon administration was overthrown after reneging on an earlier promise to handover power in 1976. The succeeding government of Murtala/Obasanjo however was committed to disengagement. It adhere strictly to its planned transition program in spite of the assassination of Murtala Mohammed in a n abortive coup in 1976. It handed over power to a civilian administration - the second republic in 1979. Our focus in this chapter is the examination of the decision of the Babangida administration-the fifth military administration (but the second since the second Republic), to hand over power to civilians in 1992.

The object of analysis ranges from whether the constantly scheduled disengagement programs are a systematic attempts to create room for mobility (political, economic and social) within the army itself, to an obvious lack of adequate accountable and responsible governing ability characterized by an absence of purposeful ideas and coherent programs. An undeniable result of military intervention in Nigerian politics is the throes of political instability in which the country finds itself - an apparent praetorian gap, whereby the military had become an opposition party.

Several reasons have been proposed for being responsible for this dilemma. The military whose primary responsibility is the security and defense of the Nation has no moral or legal justification to remove elected official, for whatever reason or to impose its decrees on the population. Military rule is undemocratic and its intervention in politics has reduced the influence and prestige of this once respected institution.

There are two basic schools of thoughts on this-namely the Janowitz and the Huntington schools-which gave reasons among others for military intervention in politics.

The Janowitz school believed that there are certain characteristics inherent in the military organization which disposes it to intervening in politics.[1] These characteristics were acquired through training and possess some other qualities such as puritanical ethic, professionalism, dedication, nationalistic ethics and in - group cohesion[2]. These qualities, according to this school not only unite the military but made it decisive.

The Huntington school on the other hand, emphasized the nature of the society within which the military exists as an important determinant of the propensity of its intervention in politics.[3] In this case, the societal and structural weaknesses and institutional fragility attracts the military to power and legitimacy vacuum. Though these two schools have been criticized for these propositions - in that the schism and fractionalization within the military as seen through coups and counter coups, runs contrary to the position of Janowitz's school while the post colonial state structure inherited the colonial state characteristics which placed the military in a position where it has enormous control of the means of coercion while its been used within the civil society to sustain and maintain power.

The existence of coups and counter coups clearly undermine the premise of military unity. The mal-administration and corruption of the military regimes also runs contrary to the afore mentioned puritanical and nationalist tendencies. Obviously, the nature of political institutions and the use to which these institutions are put to are conditioned by the modes of production, which cannot be divorced from the accumulation of capital by the dominant social class and the class struggle within that society.

The society is characterized by the gap between the rich and the poor, corruption in high places, rural-urban migration, unemployment, the erosion of institutional legitimacy, low level of social integration or and total absence of popular political participation coupled with the absence of a strong and dynamic leadership.

Other reasons given for military intervention includes, the transference of influence and ideas across boundaries - known as contagion effect; the nature of the political system and foreign intervention. The historical background of the Nigerian military is characterized by its use to suppress anti - government protesters and opposition, which is not unlike the crass flamboyance of the armies of pre-war Eastern Europe dictators[4] which resulted in its politicization. But its lack of long standing traditions and practices rendered it unable to clearly establish goals and roles it would play in a post colonial environment.

Involvement in politics in itself, imposes certain roles on the military and its response to the new demand are dictated by the nature of the military itself and its ideological orientation.

If the regime is an ideological type, it establishes upon assuming power, an ideology within which it will operate - and in most cases, these type of military regime usually ends up "civilianizing" itself or rule the country for a long time before handing over power. A good example of this is the post Nasser regime in Egypt, the regimes of Mengistu in Ethiopia and Ghadafi in Libya among others.

There is also the correctional and non strictly ideological type, which normally come into politics as an arbitrational group. They step into politics, arrest certain situations such as "mal - administration" and corruption" and reorganize the society" towards handing over to a set of civilians. They never stay for a long time and they have no clear cut ideology or goal. The Nigerian military has demonstrated these characteristics under the Murtala/Obasanjo regime(and it has become less coherent in its goal and objectives ever since), although since Babangida, the military has itself lost that clear edge of incorruptability and the potential to amend the inherent societal decay we have witnessed since independence. It has therefore become itself a central cause of the malaise.

On the question of disengagement, the military in introducing transitional programs usually buy itself time, to recruit and handover to a more sympathetic set of individuals which will normally preserve the interest of the departing officers.

They-the military leaves behind decrees and laws which make subsequent administration unable to identify, investigate and prosecute its predecessor - the military for some of its mal-administration. And if the successor is daring enough to attempt doing so, the military protects itself by engineering a coup to silence the new administration.

The Nigerian Military and Disengagement

Due to the obvious break down of law and order especially between 1964 and 1966, and due to the use of the armed forces and the police to suppress the opposition at all levels, which led to an heightened sensitization and politicization of the military, the military coup led by the five young majors, came as a welcome development on January 15th. 1966. As the first coup in Nigeria, the military was seen as the redeemer of the oppressed class in the society, liberating them from the suppressive nature and violence of the politicians of the first Republic. Not only were they seen as nationalist but as a corrective force in light of the chaos of the past years.

The abortion of the coup of the "young majors" and the emergence of General Ironsi as the beneficiary of power coupled with his attempt to unify the country(through unitary form of government) with the unification decree and the apparent dominance of the ruling and decision making apparatus of the State by the Ibos (which was construed as an Ibo attempt to hijack the governance of Nigeria, considering the fact that the first coup was led by the Ibos and the beneficiary was an Ibo - Ironsi and as a result of the coup, Northern leaders such as Tafawa Balewa - the Prime Minister was killed and Amadu Bello - the political and spiritual leader of the northern oligarchy).

It was apparent from the onset that the military exhibited the same division that permeate the society but Ironsi failed to read correctly the parallel division existing in the society. By the end of the civil war in 1970, there was a desire on the part of the people for a return to a civilian and democratic rule. This was heightened by the corrupt practices of the Gowon administration which really undermine the image of the military.

The Gowon's decision not to adhere to his original disengagement plan was seen as a betrayal of the faith the people had in the military - which prompted the coup of Murtala/Obasanjo of 1975.

The coup that ousted Gowon was not only bloodless but it brought into power new leaders who were also dedicated to handing over power to a civilian regime in 1979. The Murtala/Obasanjo administration was committed to the transition because they believed that the long military involvement in politics created a myriad of problems for the army - including problems such as, increased politicization and dissension within the top officers, unnecessary political ambitions, the quest for political offices and their quest to acquire wealth - which ultimately diverts from their primary goal of defending the country against external aggression.

This regime, which also suffered an attempted coup - which led to the assassination of Murtala Mohammed, also believed that the Gowon's corrupt, bankrupt administration and its indecision over disengagement had contributed immensely to the discrediting of the army and therefore necessitating a strict adherence on its part, to a transition program which would also curb unbridle ambition for coups and counter coups.[5] These positions were reinforced by the general opinion but the commitment of the regime led to attempted coups, among which is that of February 13th 1976 in which the then Head of State-General Murtala Mohammed was assassinated. The regime's program reinforced its commitment to reforms. It reformed the local government administration after creating more states. It created a Constituent Assembly, established the Federal Electoral Commission and a Constitutional Drafting Committee. To demonstrate its commitment to disengagement, it lifted the ban on politics and on October 1st. 1979 handed over to an elected President (Shehu Shagari). This was the first and remains the most successful transition program to civilian administration in Nigeria.

The civilian administration lasted only four years and three months, when on December 31st 1983, the coup announced by Sanni Abacha installed the administration of Buhari/Idiagbon. The administration of Shehu Shagari was condemned for its corruption, mal-administration and undermining the nation' economy. This administration never got to the point of initiating a transition program before it was removed in another coup - described as palace-coup, on August 27, 1985. The administration of Babangida that came into power following this coup initiated a disengagement program in January 1986, that would usher in a civilian administration in 1990*.

This administration encouraged a nationwide debate under the auspice of a Bureau created to study and late recommend on the form of political rule climate preferable for the third Republic in 1990. In an interview in *New African* of April 1986, General Babangida also emphasized its administration's commitment to the transition program. He said he;

> "....feel strongly, that there is a need to go back to our profession and do the job as assigned by the constitution and allow other people within the Society to run government: I feel if we have a real good system, we should be able to, in this country, have good governments without necessarily bringing the military in to do it....."[6]

This was said to have been the mind set of the senior officers like Babangida but what constitute good government and who determines whether the government is good or not. He emphasized his believe in good government and the fact that it will bring stability and progress to Nigerian society. His policies later demonstrated his lack of commitment in this wise. How can the military determine a real good government when it has an innate desire to share in the glory of being in power, living in presidential palaces, junketing from one foreign capital to the other and being addressed as the Head of this and Chief of that.

Babangida also felt that:

> "If we vote in a government and it has not done well, we should be able to hang on till the next election to vote it out..."[7]

This is a reasonable approach but as time later showed, Babangida neither believed nor was he committed to the transition program or the principles we referenced above. It is actually a reasonable approach. Political accommodation is a better solution to any misrule in a system that guarantees periodic election and if ever the military possess this spirit, one can be assure of political stability, establishment of a viable political process that will guarantee economic stability and national development.

* The date of handing over later changed in the summer of 1987 and a new date was set to be 1992. This part of the paper was initially written in 1986 and the analysis reflects the author's examination of the situation then but has been updated.

Incessant coup d'état prevent the society from evolving a culture of tolerance and political accommodation. When the military handover, it is generally back to square one - In Nigeria, the handing over in 1979, returns the country to where it stopped politically(cryogenized) in 1966 with regionally based political parties and leadership and the trend was about to be broken in 1993 until the Babangida annulment of the election that almost install M.K.O. Abiola as the President in the Third Republic.

Babangida also hoped that:

> "....that ours(military his administration) will probably be the last intervention of the military in the political system in the country?"[8]

His hope never materialized because his defense chief is currently the head of State after removing the transition government that he (Babangida) had handed over to a few months earlier in 1993.

Praetorian Gap

The Nigerian society can aptly be described has haven fallen into a praetorian gap - a constant recurrence of military intervention in politics - where non intervention cannot be guaranteed in the future of the country. Among the factors responsible for this includes the ambition of junior officers, which has led to denial of service to some still able and experienced military officers or their forced retirement and dismissal. This enabled the young and ambitious officer to entrench their leadership. Nigeria for example have the largest number of young generals, with most retired at the age of 40. Another factor is the irresponsible civilian leadership which usually create political unrest and the break down of law and order thereby creating the conditions necessary for military intervention.

The military has evolved into an alternative political force since the nationalist parties went into decline in the immediate post independence years.[9] While it was easy for the military to seize power it became more and more difficult to govern because the strength of the military also accounts for its basic weakness. The use of weapons internally erodes the confidence of the masses in the army. Though military efficiency can accomplish technical task, it does not relate to the calculation of social choices and balancing of social interests.

As the military strive to govern, it found itself shifting from management to bargaining, a pattern that subjects officers to political pressures with which they are all ill equipped to deal with as military men. The Babangida's administration clearly demonstrated these inadequacies.

After the national debate of 1992 on the International Monetary Fund (IMF) and membership of the Organization of Islamic Congress (OIC), the government came became less tolerant and suppress students, workers and university professors. It banned trade unions and close universities and banned newspapers. Not only does the military lost its human right record but its credibility nationally and internationally.

The administration however declared its commitment to the transition time table which looked like this:

1987: Establishment of:
The Directorate of Social Mobilization
The national Electoral Commission
The Constitutional Drafting Committee
The elections into the local governments on non-party basis.
1988: Establishment of:
The National Population Commission
The Code of Conduct Tribunal
The Constituent Assembly
The Inauguration of National Revenue Mobilization Commission.
Termination of structural Adjustment Program(SAP)
Consolidation of the gains of Adjustment Program(SAP)
1989: Promulgation of a New Constitution
Release of New Fiscal Arrangements.
Lift of ban on Part Politics
Announcement of two recognized and registered
Political parties
Election into local governments on Political party basis.
1990: Election into State legislatures and State Executives.
Convening of State Legislatures
Swearing -in of State Executives.
1991: Census
Local Government Elections

1992: Election into Federal legislatures and Conveying
National Assembly
Presidential election, swearing-in of New President
And final disengagement by the Armed forces.

It was suppose to be a gradual disengagement and it started off that way but the date changed and the final transition was scheduled to be in June 1993. The two parties that were registered the Social Democratic Party - with Moshood Abiola as the Party Presidential candidate and the National Republican Party led by Bashir Othman Tofa. Abiola was leading in the election when the result was annulled. The election of June 13, 1993 marked an important milestone in the political history of Nigeria. M.K. O Abiola, a southerner but a Moslem, close to the military was on his way to winning with votes from many part of the country which seems like a departure from earlier pattern of political trend.

Babangida ignored strikes, riots and international condemnation that resulted from the election annulment but he was forced to step down but Sanni Abacha toppled the business man he appointed as his successor. The new government of Sanni Abacha in his turn promise a return to civilian administration. The impasse that Nigeria has found itself continue to undermine the country's standing even five years after the annulment. As a southern Yoruba, Abiola was considered a threat to the dominance of the northern Hausa-Fulani. This position like many others could be challenged because it was in the same north that he defeated his northern opponent in the election. Many also said, the military just wasn't ready to disengagement.

The strikes, riots and international condemnation that resulted from the election annulment created such turmoil that Babangida was forced to step down and when Abacha toppled his successor, Ernest Shonekan, he dissolved all elected legislatures and forced Babangida's top military allies to retire. Although promising a return to democracy, Abacha jailed activists and reporters who criticized him. In fact the environmental and human rights activist - Ken Sarowiwa and many other of his followers were hanged under his watch. Recently Gen. Shehu Musa Yar'Adua, the no.2 man in the military government that ceded power to civilians in 1979 was jailed and died recently in prison. Gen Obasanjo a retired head of state and M.K.O Abiola remain in prison.

On April 22, Abacha announced his government's transition program and five days later inaugurated the National Constitutional Conference Electoral

Committee. At the anniversary of the annulled election, MKO Abiola came back into the country trying to assume his presidential mandate and Abacha in response reaffirmed his government commitment to disengagement. According to him, " no individual or group will be permitted to hold this country to ransom. We have had enough and we have seen enough. Everywhere men in Nigeria condemn the attempt of some individuals and groups seeking to translate their personal ambition into a national trauma"[10]. Gen. Abacha could be talking about his government as well as he was trying to warn MKO Abiola. He later arrested Abiola and he has been in prison ever since.

CONCLUSION

The transition program of Abacha is in place and the country is moving slowly towards democratic transition, with the election of a President in the fall of 1998. That President could be Abacha, who is being primed to be the candidate and civilian President - a la Rawlings in Ghana, by the end of the year. In 1997, his government came up with the current transition program and it must be said that its proceeding slowly but the trust of the people in its success is very low - shown by the low election turn out in the past election. The ambivalence of the people is understandable in light of previous experience. The Abacha plan started with:

1995 - Approved constitution and establishment of National Electoral Commission and the lifting of restrictions on political activities.

1996 - Witnessed the inauguration and election into local government on non - party basis and the creation of states and local governments - the number of states increased to 33. Followed by party registration and election into local governments on party basis. The five parties approved by Abacha were the Democratic Part of Nigeria led by Alhaji Sule Ahmed; Grassroots Democratic Movement led by Alhaji Gambo Lawan; Congress For National Consensus led by Dr Abel Ubeku; United Nigeria congress Party led by Alhaji Isa Mohammed and National Centre Party of Nigeria led by Alhaji Magaji Abdullahi.

The program also scheduled the inauguration of elected local government officials and party state primaries to select candidates for state assembly and governorship election for 1997. The election of state governors was scheduled for the fourth quarter of 1997. The year 1998 remains the pivotal year of this program because, scheduled for this period are the inauguration of State Assembly and governors, party primaries for national assembly elections, national assembly campaigns and elections and the primaries to select candidates for presidential elections, the campaigns for presidential elections, the presidential elections, the swearing - in of the elected president and final disengagement. It is the hope of many in Nigeria and around the world that this transition will bring sanity and political stability to this country. It is however difficult to expect that this will be the end of military involvement in politics, given the experience since independence and the fact that the military in Nigeria has turned itself into an opposition to the civilians and would be ready to jump into politics as situation presents itself. This will not be the last transition program, it is just one of many to come.

Notes

1) Janowitz M (1964)*The Military in Political Development of New Nations* (Chicago: University of Chicago Press, p.45)
2) Ibid
3) Huntington S.P.(1967)The Soldiers and the State (Cambridge, Mass.: Havard University Press)
4) See Falola T & Ihonvbere J (1985)The Rise and Fall of Nigeria's 2nd Republic (1979-1984) (London, Zed Books)
5) Brice B, "The Nature and Role of the Military in Sub - Sahara Africa" Africa Forum Vol.2 No: Summer 1966) p.57
6) See Falola T and Ihonvbere J. op cit.
7) Guardian, Lagos: Sunday, March 30, 1986.
8) Ibid
9) Ibid and see Finer, S.E. The Man on Horse Back (London, Pall Mall Press, 1962) and Janowitz M op cit. P.74

See also Bell J.W, (1965) "Army and nations in Sub-Sahara Africa" in Adelphi Papers No: 21, Aug. 1965.

Chapter Four

MANAGING NIGERIA'S ECONOMIC SYSTEM IN THE THIRD REPUBLIC

Adepoju Adeleke

INTRODUCTION

The five basic functions of management are generally identified as planning, organizing, mobilizing resources, directing and controlling the activities of men and machines towards the attainment of some objectives. The formulation of objectives is in addition considered an essential function of management. The exercise of these functions puts the manager in a decision situation. one way or the other, management is involved in decision making, and decision making involves problem solving. Generally, a decision situation exists when: there is a desired objectives, alternative courses of actions are available, there is uncertainty as to which course is best, and external factors are present which are outside the control of the decision maker.

The choosing of any course of action involves management in problem solving. Problem solving therefore has traditionally been taken as an essential function of management.

In an economy/country, two principal actors are normally involved in the management and control of the economy. These are the government and individuals sometimes acting as cooperate bodies. The degree of management and control of each of the actors depend on the economic system adopted in such an economy/country. A country's economic system therefore, is the way the economic problems of planning, organizing, controlling, coordinating, and harnessing of the resources of the country are solved. Different economies/countries have adopted different economic systems in the management of their economic system. Whatever the system is adopted, a number of things are common to each of them. First, there are factors of production; the factors are owned, the factors are combined in certain ways, the output is distributed and consumed. In the process, some surplus is left unconsumed. This is invested to form the basis for future consumption.

Whatever economic system is operated in a country, answers to the following principal questions are necessary in the management of the economy:

Who should own the factors of production?

How should the production output be distributed?

How should the surplus that results from output being greater than consumption distributed?

Quite a number of economic systems have been tried to solve the problem of managing the economic system at different times since the existence of man on earth. These systems include feudalism, mercantilism, colonialism, slavery, communism, socialism, etc. In the world today, the dominant systems are capitalism and socialism. There are varieties of each of these two economic systems. At one end is pure capitalism in which all the factors of production are owned by the capitalist, who makes all the investment decisions and receives all the profits of the investment. Under capitalism, the workers supply the labor and receive wages which would depend on their trade unions' ability to negotiate with the owners.

At the other extreme is communism in which all the factors of production are owned by the people (represented by a centralized government), and they make the investments and provide the labor. The profits from the investments theoretically accrue to the people, and are expected to be shared according to the needs of the people.

Pure capitalism and pure communism cannot, in reality, exist. Thus, we have varieties of mixed economic systems in which the government and the capitalist co-exist. What the capitalist control is called the private sector of the economy and what the government controls is called the public sector. Under socialism, the government owns a large proportion of the factors of production and employs the workers who are paid wages according to their contribution. The profits-surplus thus accrues to the government, who uses it on behalf of the people.

Economic Systems in Nigeria Before 1972

Over the years, different economic systems have been practiced in Nigeria. In the olden days, before the advent of colonial era, the economic system adopted in Nigeria was a sort of communism. By this system, the factors of production were land and labor. The land was communally owned and was held in trust for the people by the head of the commune and was divided among the families in the village. The labor was owned and supplied by the family. The productive process pursued was agriculture and the output consumed was agricultural product. What was not consumed was saved and planted (invested) during the next season.

The output usually varied according to the size of the family. Consumption also depended on the size of the family. Whatever was left out of output which was not consumed became a surplus that accrued to the whole family. Where there was a head chief or head of family, part of the surplus was paid to him.

When the British rule started in Nigeria, another economic system emerged. The economy was mainly agrarian and the colonial government claimed ownership of some of the factors of production-mainly things below the surface of the ground.

To this end, part of the surplus accrued to the colonial government and this was transferred out of the country. This formed a leakage from the economy. The advent of the Europeans also brought foreign investors into the country. These investors established subsidiary companies in Nigeria with headquarters in the home countries overseas. These subsidiary companies (who were in fact multinationals) were involved in trading: bringing into the country such manufactured goods as drinks, clothing materials, gun powder, cigarette, building materials, and stationaries. They bought from Nigerians agricultural products such as palm kernels, cotton, cola nuts, hides and skin, groundnuts and some other products. They often repatriate the surpluses accruing from their businesses to the home countries.

To a large extent, the management of the private sector of the economy was dominated by these multinationals. This system was in operation some years after the country became independent in 1960.

The Indigenization of 1972 and After

Some years after political independence, it became clear to Nigerians that political independence, for it to be meaningful, should be founded on a bedrock of economic independence. It was in the realization of this fact that in March 1972, the Nigerian government promulgated the Indigenization Decree. The decree compels some foreign business organizations to share the ownership of some of their business interests with Nigerians. Since 1972, other similar decrees have been promulgated, the most important of them being the decree of January 12, 1977.

The decree classified all enterprises in Nigeria into three schedules:

Schedule 1 consists of enterprises which should be 100 percent owned and managed exclusively by Nigerians;

Schedule 2 are enterprises where Nigerians should acquire up to 60 percent equity participation; while,

Schedule 3 consists of enterprises with 40 percent equity participation by Nigerians.

The decree then stipulated that appropriate equities of those enterprises were to be sold or transferred to Nigerians not later than December 31 1978 (or June 30 1977 for some classes of businesses).

The principal objective of the indigenization decree therefore is to transfer the management of the Nigerian economy from expatriate domination to indigenous Nigerians. Thus, the decrees of 1972 and 1977 whatever may be their shortcomings, effected not only a change of ownership but also that of management of the Nigerian economy.

Some Policy Considerations for the Effective Management of the Nigerian Economic System In The Third Republic

According to the political program of the present military administration, the third republic for Nigeria will commence as from 1 October 1992, when hopefully the military government will hand over power to an elected civilian administration. The principal questions to ask are: who should do the management of the Nigerian economy and how should it be managed in the third republic?

The first question appears to have been answered by the Indigenization decrees. That is, Nigerians forming public or private liability companies, partnership or further still sole proprietorship should be, by and large involved in the management of the economy. Multinationals with appropriate equity participation of Nigerians should also be involved in the management of the economy. This suggestion tend to attribute a greater percentage of the management of the economy to the private sector. This seems to be the spirit of the indigenization policy.

This policy should be allowed to operate in the overall interest of the nation. It is a free enterprise (laissez faire) policy which means minimum intervention of government and greater participation of private individuals in business management.

The management of the economy involves decision making, and decision making for effective management involves skill, precision, dynamism, risk-taking, foresight and entrepreneurship; government red-tape administrative process, bureaucracy, and the maintenance of status quo characteristics of public administration would not augur well for the rapid transformation and the effective management of the economy.

There is no system that has no limitation, however, the living experiences of the development gap between countries that adopt a free enterprise system and those that operate a government centrally controlled and managed economy is a pointer that the later *does not allow* for effective development of the economy. It is observed for example, that most countries of Western Europe that adopt free enterprise system in the management of their economy are better able to develop economically than their Eastern Europe counterparts whose economic system are centrally controlled and managed by the government.

Under the free enterprise system, Nigerians acting as corporate bodies or single individuals make nearly all the investment decisions in the economy, and also receive all the profits which accrue from their investment decisions while paying taxes to government. Workers supply the labor and receive wages which would depend on their trade unions' ability to negotiate with the owners and management of the enterprises. Government involvement in the management of the economy should be reduced to a minimum level.

Under this situation, the economic model that emerge could be depicted as follows - see figure 1 (p. 94); In which a greater percentage of investment decisions are made by Nigerians operating as individuals or as cooperate bodies. In the figure 1, some percentages of the total economy is reserved for the control and management of foreigners acting as multinationals. This structure upholds the spirit of the indigenization decree. This is because there are some areas of businesses which involve heavy capital outlay or high level technology for which Nigerians have not acquired the necessary capabilities and know how. Such areas of businesses should be left for the multinationals to operate. They should however go into these areas with appropriate equity participation of Nigerians as stipulated in the policy of indigenization. This is necessary because no country can develop all alone. It is pertinent therefore, to allow for flow of information, capital, ideas and technological know how. The multinationals, with their wealth of business acumen and know how would bring in these essential factors of economic development. Upon all, it is suggested that foreign investors should be encouraged to participate in the sectors of the economy which have been allocated to them in the indigenization decree.

The second question is thus answered. The distribution of production output should be left to the free interplay of demand and supply characteristics of free market economy.

What role for government in the management of the economy in the third republic? It is observed that the functions of government in any economy are to:

1. make laws and regulations -- - legislative functions
2. interpret laws and regulations -- - judiciary functions
3. execute laws and regulations -- - executive functions.

We tend to suggest that the Nigerian third republic government should limit its role to these areas as far as possible for the reasons which have been advanced above. Under this situation governments either at state or federal level should sell off some of the shares which they have acquired in the profit making enterprises in Nigeria. These shares should be sold to indigenous Nigerians.

However, government should be involved in infrastructural developments which are indispensable for economic development. These include uninterrupted electric supply, efficient network of roads, effective health care delivery system, effective telecommunications systems, portable water for domestic and industrial uses, air and sea ports, and other social services. In other to meet these challenges, government should set up effective machinery for revenue collection from the private and corporate business enterprises.

The government should also be responsible for formulating and implementing educational policies. However, private bodies who want to participate in the implementation of the educational policies should be allowed to do so at the primary and secondary level of the educational system. This will reduce the burden on the government's shoulder in view of the demographic profile of the country which is characterized by young population. It will be necessary however for the government to set necessary standards for the educational system.

In the industrial relations sphere, the role of government should be that of an impartial judge between labor unions and the management of business enterprises. We have earlier suggested (see Adeleke 1984) that government should uphold the doctrine of laissez-faire in industrial relations matters in Nigeria. The laissez-faire principle gives an individual the opportunity to enter into a free contractual relationship with whoever decides to employ him. This principle is based on the "Benthamite Utilitarian" principle that an individual who knows best his interest should be left free to pursue and maximize those interests, the sum total of which for the society as a whole would be greater good of the greatest number.

Laissez-faire also means that the government should assist both employers and unions to treat themselves as they thought best with themselves. It has also been said that the most effective way to having and maintaining industrial peace and harmony is for both employees and employers or their representatives to freely enter into contractual relationships through collective bargaining without intervention, involvement nor interference of any third party. According to the United Committee of Central Labor Organization (UCLO 1970), the best form of salary structure and salaries and wages revision would be that evolved by the two sides in industry: labor and management through collective bargaining.

It has however been recognized that for collective bargaining to be really free and effective, it is essential for the bargaining strength of both employees and employers to be as far as possible equally matched. Fawehinmi(1976) suggested that one of the ways for achieving this is for the government to strengthen the capabilities of weaker party (usually the labor unions) so that they can bargain on equal footing with the employers. The principle of having equal capability is based on the Asby's (1964) Law of Requisite Variety.

That "ONLY VARIETY ABSORBS VARIETY" i.e. 'iron sharpens iron'.... In figure 2 below, the role of government in the industrial relations system in the third republic is to amplify the capacity of the unions (employees) so that they can have equal bargaining power with that of the employers(management).See Figure 2: The Role of Government in The Nigeria's Industrial Relations System In The Third Republic (page 94 below). on the other hand, government should reduce the excesses of employers (management) so that they will be able and willing to negotiate with unions. The role of government as far as this suggestion is concerned is reduced to that of variety engineering, and maintaining the balance of power between the parties. In making this suggestion, government is being looked at as the supreme authority of the state and not that of government as the owner of investments and the overall employer of labor.

The most effective ways to maintain this balance of power is for government to enact laws which could make collective bargaining and joint consultation effective in work environment. Such laws would determine the scope, functions, structure and methods of operations of the agreements as may be appropriate to the conditions in the various undertakings. Having presented what should be the role of government in the management of the Nigerian economy in the third republic, we consider it necessary to discuss some basic principles towards the management of the economy.

Some Principles for the Management of the Nigerian Economy

Since the time of Taylor(1911), or rather before him, it has been recognized that there are approaches (principles) for the effective management of an Organization or an economy. It was in recognition of this truism that Taylor proposed his famous "Principles of Scientific Management". The author observed through a series of simple illustrations both at the national level and the private level where he was a foreman of a steel company that the whole country (U.S.A) was suffering from a great loss due to inefficiency in the production processes.

Taylor then proposed that the inefficiency can be reduced or eliminated through a scientific principles of management. The dominating interests of the author was how the Organization could be made more efficient. In arriving at proposing a "Scientific Principle of Management", Taylor conducted a time and motion studies to determine how tasks should be organized towards increased productivity. He observed that rests periods during the working day were necessary in order to recover from psychological fatigue. The author conceived man (employee) as an economic man that can only be motivated by wages and incentives pays.

Although, the scientific management approach dealt almost exclusively with the production structure of the Organization, and little to say about the institutional and managerial structures of an Organization, the approach seem to offer an insight into how tasks can be organized for productive efficiency. The Nigerian Managers have a lot to benefit from Taylor's proposition of a scientific approach to management of an Organization.

The industrial relations approach to management pioneered by Elton Mayo and his colleagues (1927-1933) at Hawthorne in USA ended up by emphasizing the importance of interpersonal and group relations as a factor of organizational efficiency. The approach sees people in Organization not merely as individuals responding to the formal requirements of their roles, but as group members developing their own norms and their own cohesion. They therefore work in Organization partly to satisfy their social needs and not mainly for economic gains.

As a result of the studies of Mayo and his colleagues, the industrial relations approach to management lay emphasis on people in Organization and their motivation as important factors of organizational effectiveness. It has been observed that one of the methods for managing business concerns or any Organization for that matter for effectiveness is also by "Management by Objectives". Drucker(1968), noted that Management by Objectives (MBO) is a principle of management that gives common direction of vision and effort, establish team work and harmonize the goals of the individual with the common goal. For Ejiofor(1981), Management by objectives is a method of management whereby the superior and subordinate managers of an Organization agree on its broad goals, translate these goals into a chain of specific short-term goals, define each individual's major areas of responsibility in terms of results expected, continually review the accomplishment of the subordinate, and use goals accomplishment as the sole basis of accessing and rewarding the subordinate.

From this conception, Management by Objectives has five key features:

1 organizational or departmental goals are jointly set by the manager and his superior,
2 Broad long-term goals are translated into a chain of specific interrelated short term goals,
3 Continual guidance of subordinate by superior,
4 Continual review of accomplishment by subordinate and superior,
5 Contribution towards goal achievement serves as sole basis of subordinate rewards.

The ultimate objective of MBO is to increase the effectiveness and efficiency of an organization through optimum performance of its members. This is realized by making all members of an organization committed to achieving the organizational objectives.

Another approach to management is the systems approach. This approach to management of an organization or an economy is an emerging paradigm for inquiring into the complexly of social, managerial, organizational and technological problems of a given situation. The approach starts with the definition of objectives, and ends with the implementation of the objectives. It gives a description or a design of an harmonious optimum ensemble of the required men and machines with such a corollary network of flow of information and materials needed to operate in order to achieve the given objectives.

The basic notion of a system is simply that it is a set of inter-related parts. Implicit in these concepts is a degree of wholeness which makes the whole something different from, and more than the individual units considered separately. The systems approach emphasizes looking at a problem in its entirety, taking into account all the interdependent parameters. It is a process for understanding how those parameters interact with one another and how they can be brought into proper relationships for attaining the given objectives.

It is noted that no system, existing either as an economy or an organization exists in an isolation. A system normally exist in an environment which in itself exist in a larger environment. An understanding of the strength and weakness of the larger environment is therefore imperative for effective management of the system.

To be effective, managers in the Nigerian economic system must understand organization-environment relationships. They must take cognizance of the ways organizations are tied to other structures - the political influences, technological developments, global world economies and markets, and societal values. An understanding of these phenomenon is likely to offer the managers a knowledge of the relationships which their organizations will require to assure their own survival in the complex environment in which they operate. The system approach provides an insight on how to manage complex organizations in an environment.

Which management principle is appropriate for Nigeria in the management of the economy in the third republic?

The Japanese have risen to become a world economic power of our time. One of the factors which have helped the Japanese is partly their approach to management of organizations. This approach is based solidly on the cultural values of the Japanese people - love of Japan, organizational and job commitment, trust, cooperation, collective decision making, collective responsibility and rewards, implicit controls, holistic relationship, tolerance of ambiguity and emphasis on interdependency. The processes and issues which underline these are essential to cooperative and productive effort.

One of the distinctive features of Japanese management philosophy is not so much of basic skills transfer but of sharing of organizational philosophies, values and beliefs which of course are based on the society's values and aspirations.

As we move towards 1992, the era of the third republic, Nigerians have a lot to learn from the Japanese experience in the management of the economy for effectiveness.

First, a more concerted effort is needed to understand our culture from the perspective of how it enhances or hinders productive efforts. To do so will require an in depth study of our traditional social institutions and values. From the studies, we will be able to evolve a management philosophy appropriate to our environment and which enhances productive efforts and organizational effectiveness. In fact, Nigerians must be prepared to learn in the third republic.

CONCLUSION

The implications of this chapter for better management of the Nigeria's economic system can be summarized four sentences. First, to a large extent, the ownership, control and management of business organizations in Nigeria should be left in the hands of Nigerians operating either as an individual or corporate bodies. Second, the government should uphold the principles of laissez-faire in industries consisting of the total economy. Third, collective bargaining should be allowed to operate in industry. Fourth, Nigerians who are involved in the management of the economy must be prepared to learn in the third republic.

Over the years, the determinants of operational performance and effectiveness of an economy has been a subject of several studies. In this chapter we offer suggestions which might usher in a new era of self reliance and effective performance of the Nigerian economy. We observe that our suggestions are in line with the current global thinking on how an economic system can be managed in the overall interest of the society. It is hoped that the implementation of these suggestions would lead to an improved performance of the Nigerian's economic system in the third republic.

NOTES

Adeleke A (1984): "The Role of Government in the Nigerian Industrial Relations Systems: A Critical View" in Hashim I (ed): *Issues in Public Sector Management In Nigeria* (Zaria: Nigeria: Ahmadu Bello University Press Ltd.)

Ashby R (1964): *An Introduction to Cycbernetics*_(London: Menthien and Co Ltd)

Drucker P.F *(1968): The Practice of Management* (London: Pan Books Ltd).

Ejiofor P (1981): *Management in Nigeria: Theories and Issues* (Onitsha, Nigeria:African Educational Publishers (Nig) Ltd.) Fawehinmi M.A.(1967): "Industrial Relations In Nigeria"

Paper presented at a *10-day National Seminar* on *Labor Management* organized by the Nigerian Workers Council, British Council, Ibadan: Nigeria

Mayo E *(1933)*: *The Human Problems of an Industrial Civilization* (New York: Macmillan).

Taylor F.W (1923): *The Principles of Scientific Management (*New York: Harper and Row)

The Nigerian Enterprises Promotion Decree 1972, Decree No 4

The Nigerian Enterprises Promotion Decree 1977, Decree No 3

United Committee of Central Labor Organization (UCLO) 1970

"Equitable Demands for Economic Growth and National Prosperity" *Memorandum No 123* (Geneva)

Chapter Five

THE THIRD REPUBLIC AND NIGERIA'S FOREIGN POLICY OPTIONS

Aderemi Ajibewa

The aim of this chapter is to examine briefly the trend, contradictions and achievements of Nigeria's foreign policy since Independence, from Tafawa Balewa, through the Gowon, Murtala Mohammed, Shagari, Buhari to Babangida regimes - the Shonekan and Abacha regimes that followed continue the same policy but the Abacha regime suffered from the sanctions resulting from the hanging of Ken Sarowiwa and international condemnation from the continue violations of human rights (with Abiola, Obasanjo and many others in prison) and at the same time continue its ambitious policy in West Africa through the use of ECOMOG in Liberia and sierra Leone.

However, a short summary of the legacy of the First and Second Republic, and the almost 28 years of military rule might be useful exercise for projecting the foreign policy of the Third Republic in Nigeria.

We all know from Nigeria history that while politicians may have been less than impressive, military rule has not been a repository of good tidings. Coup plotters have shown themselves not to be professional military men but the politician in military uniforms intent on achieving their ultimate political ambition and have only gained power through the machinery of force. The West African region is now an assembly of military dictators and military turncoats. Given his own assessment of the coup and counter-coup syndrome that has become endemic in Nigeria, General Babangida opined that "It may be that our origin as a colonial force, our sudden and rapid expansion, that the fact that the forces have had little experience of civil authority and control, our frequent exposure to political roles, the decision not to honor fully the military tradition at the end of the civil war and, the lack of deep-rooted national military tradition due to the absence of long - serving superior officers may all have eroded our professional values"[1].

However, 1986, gave cause for hope when, in September, a Political Bureau was Bet up, thus setting the scene for a transfer of power to an elected civilian regime. In addition, the President argued that "good governance" is the antidote to coup d'état, hence, if the proper foundation is laid through the transitional program, his would be the last military regime in Nigeria.

THE FOUNDATION OF NIGERIA'S FOREIGN POLICY

There has since independence been unconcealed awareness of the historical and geographical fact that Nigeria belongs to Africa and a conviction in what Dr. Nnamdi Azikwe, who had been closely associated with Pan-Africanism since 1945, called " the historic and manifest destiny of Nigeria on the African continent"[2]. The belief appears to be that, before the birth of Nigeria, Africa was a continent drifting on an uncharted ocean. Nigeria's responsibility to Africa and to the World is to find the destination of the drifting continent. Thus Africa has been declared the center-piece of Nigeria's foreign policy by successive regimes since her independence.

Indeed, in a statement to the House of Representative, the Prime Minister Tafawa Balewa laid down the cardinal principles of his foreign policy as promotion of national interest; remaining with Commonwealth because "all its members are autonomous communities equal in status" and would greatly benefit from their interchange of ideas; not associating as a matter of routine, with any of the Power blocs, lest freedom of action be curtailed; feeding and fostering understanding and forging cultural and economic links among the African states; and by being the member of the United Nation directing her energy to influence the course of events in World affairs towards peace[3].

These objectives and principles have remained constant despite Nigeria's momentous and dramatic experiences on the domestic and international scene. However, successive administrations in Nigeria have paid much attention to the formulation and articulation of foreign policy positions and very little to the administration of the totality of the country's external relations. Therefore, in the Third Republic, the principles and objectives do not need reformulation; rather what is needed is an intensification of efforts to achieve the objectives.

Also, the problems of management, coordination and control within the Foreign Ministry, and between it and the other Ministries and government agencies have to be seriously addressed.

Nevertheless, aspiration is one thing, and its achievement another. Many a time the gap between the two is unbridgeable, because a foreign policy depends largely upon the internal situation in a country. The non governmental elitė or articulate public criticized the government of the First Republic in Nigeria for its lack of a dynamic foreign policy especially on issues such as the handling of the Congo crisis, membership in the Monrovia Bloc, decolonization and anti-apartheid. Thus Balewa government was considered by its critics as one that was out of step with progressive opinion in Africa" and for being too pro - west in its foreign policy orientations[4].

Party politics during the First Republic, however, was distinguished by its pluralism and institutionally expressed by a vibrant multi-party system.

The period of the first military intervention (1966-1979) coincided with the period of the oil boom. The bulk of the Nigerian crude oil - a resources which accounted for nearly 95.0 percent of Nigerian export earning[5], went a long way to boost the foreign policy posture of the military regime. The military government of Murtala Mohammed/Obasanjo was, however, widely regarded as having pursued a dynamic foreign policy, in that for the first time Nigeria took a highly principled stand on the issue of central concern to African nations - recognition

of the MPLA and the Beating of Angola in the OAU, nationalization of the assets of the British Petroleum in order to induce Margaret Thatcher to agree to the independence of Zimbabwe under the leadership of Mugabe instead of Bishop Muzorewa [6].The last civilian regime under President Shehu Shagari did not fully make the Africa the center of Nigeria's foreign policy. Quite frankly, since nothing was basically wrong with the 1979 constitution other than its operators, it might perhaps be necessary to examine the Second Republic Constitutional provision on Foreign policy and Nigeria's foreign policy under the Second Republic.

Constitutional Provisions on Foreign Policy

Giving all the apparent confused and even conflicting postures of the various Political parties in the Second Republic and the two recognized ones for the Third Republic, we would as a matter of need be interested in knowing what the constitution says about the foreign policy posture of the country.

Unlike the previous constitutions, the 1979 constitution contains some sections dealing with foreign policy objectives[7]. The foreign policy formulation as guided by the principles laid down and reinforced by the Adedeji Report on Nigeria's foreign relations was to continue guiding the formulation of policies. These principles are, the defense of territorial integrity and independence of the country, the establishment of the necessary and economic coalition, the promotion of equality and self - reliance in Africa with respect for human dignity especially for Black people as well as the defense and promotion of world peace.

While these are sound objectives, most of them are not practicable and therefore, cannot provide a rational and realistic basis for the country's external behavior. Indeed, some of these objectives such as the promotion of equality and self - reliance in Africa and the creation of necessary political and economic conditions in Africa are beyond the capability of Nigeria. The constitution dealt with the executive and political dimension of the presidential role in foreign policy.

As the Commander in Chief of the armed forces and the chief executive[8], the President had an unprecedented opportunity to direct the country's external affairs, as a chief formulator and spoke person and executor of all legislation and programs dealing with foreign policy as well as the chief defender of Nigeria's territorial integrity and security. Only the President received foreign ambassadors and diplomatic Message. He also appointed Nigeria's ambassadors and a minister of external affairs with ratification of the Senate. For the conduction and initiation of foreign policy, the position of the President was much more implicated than the constitution implied.

For instance, any treaty entered into with foreign countries by the President must first be ratified by the National Assembly[9]. He could not declare war unilaterally without informing the National Assembly and he could not deploy Nigerian troops to combat without Senate approval.[10] The constitution was drafted by the ruling class, hence the constitution mirrored the behavior of the ruling elite. This being the case, the constitution could not serve the interest of the majority since it was actually designed for the ruling minority. If foreign policy is to be rational, it must serve the interest of the people from whose taxes the government is financed and maintained.

It would be pertinent for us to examine a brief transitional process established by Babangida regime. The banning of the old politician had not succeeded in purging Nigeria's body politic. Nor has the system of government sponsored political parties, The National Republican Convention (NRC) and, the Social Democratic Parties (SDP) with their nearly identical manifesto-inspired analysts with hope for dynamic political debate nor aggressive foreign policy. Typical cases of blatant rigging accusations, protests, and high handedness abounds in many states. Many reasons have, however been advanced as being responsible for this trend.

Surprisingly, the banned old politicians whose unseen hands attempt to control the new generation politicians have sponsored their proteges. Complains and petitions reached such as alarming proportion that a presidential candidate, Otunba Olabiyi Durojaiye sent a philosophical warning "Unless we develop the courage to avoid rigging and to accept the wishes of the people the stability of the third Republic will be in jeopardy"[11].

Prof. Adebayo Adedeji, formerly the Executive Secretary of the Economic Commission for Africa (ECA) prior to the election, have also put it simply as, how we conduct politics during the transition program will determine whether it will be a bouncing baby or a still-born baby. And if we define the new breed to mean old wine in new bottles, then we will have spelt the doom of the new Republic even before it comes into existence.[12]

However, against the above background, the President had to suspend the handing over till August 1993.

Nigerian Foreign Policy under the Second Republic, 1979-83

It was on the basis Of the constitution that the 1979 elections were conducted and culminated in the enthronement of Alhaji Shehu Shagari as the President on October 1, 1979. However, the Presidential candidate in his campaign declared that a creditable defense of the territorial integrity of Nigeria would be among the main aim and objectives of his party, the National Party of Nigeria. He further added that he would promote the "enlightened foreign policy which seeks the best interest of Nigeria and World peace and orderliness"[13]

In October 1979, when the Shagari government came to office, there was over $ 9 billion in foreign reserves.[14] Crude oil export was over 2 million barrels a day, and the price reached the all - time high of $ 44.36 a barrel in January, 1980 largely as a result of the outbreak of the Gulf war. Shagari administration did not attempt to diversify the economy. The enormous earnings from the crude oil was not used to strengthen the economy, rather it was squandered on the importation of consumer goods, luxury projects and festivals and on expensive frivolous sometimes adventitious foreign policy. The end result was a balance of payment deficit, and the accumulation of debts. Thus, in 1981, there was a balance of payment deficit of N3.036.8 million(N'Naira). In 1982, the corresponding figure was N5.2 billion and in 1983, it was a deficit of N3.4 billion[15]. This led directly to the run - down of the foreign reserves. From about N6.5 billion in 1982, and to N819 million in December 1983. External debt rose from just N0.5 billion in December 1979 to over N8.30 billion[16] in December 1983. Internal debt rose from N3.0 billion in 1979 to over N22 billion in December 1983.

The consequences of all these for the country's foreign policy were serious.

While in the period before the collapse of the oil market in 1981, Shagari government had been threatening the Western powers with the use of oil as a weapon over increasing American connection with South Africa under President Reagan.

However, since January 1981 onwards, the government had to tone down its rhetoric to secure the American support for the International Monetary Fund (IMF) loan for which Nigerian government applied by early 1982. Indeed, the Shagari government stopped the attempt of the Nigerian Senate from discussing the American invasion of Grenada late in 1983.[17] Criticism of other Western powers by the Shagari government became muted and mild even on African issues such as military and economic ties with South Africa. However, the government to found alternative markets for its oil in some Communist States.[18] The withdrawal of recognition from the PAC, and the SARYCO and the closing of their offices in Lagos, Nigeria, were largely due to the desire to make some financial savings. The massive expulsion of over 2 million illegal aliens from Nigeria by January 1983, was due largely to the economic predicament of the country and was criticized by the press and undermine the foreign policy posture of the Second Republic.

The government's freedom of maneuver in foreign policy would however, be assessed in selected critical issues, especially the administration's relation with Chad, Cameroun, Israel, the O.A.U. It must, be stressed from the onset that the press plays a considerable role in the foreign policy process. It is the press that informs the public about changes in the external political environment. It also relays information about wars, disasters, elections, and other happenings which might have implications for the rest Of the world. More often than not, the press is the only source of information for policy formulation.

The task is also to measure performance against promises by constantly evaluating what statesmen do against what they propose to do especially during critical times such as international crises and at election years. They also act as a watch-dog against arbitrary positions, procedures or practices within the foreign policy making structure. By discharging these tasks, the press say, therefore provide a check on government and ensure that the government does not over step its bonds.

NIGERIA-CHADIAN RELATIONS

Nigeria got involved with Chadian crisis because of ethno-cultural similarities and the imperative for national security. The French and Libyan factors, however, as well as refugee problems, made it unavoidable for Nigeria to become interested in developments in Chad.

Nigeria's worst diplomatic reverse was suffered in Chad. The reverse were in terms of direct humiliation and disgrace which Nigeria's and its armed forces suffered at the hands of Chadian factions for the first time under the military in 1979. Further humiliation of Nigeria and its armed forces was suffered under Shagari administration, when Nigerian armed forces went to Chad as part of the OAU peace keeping forces in December 1981 until June 1982 simply to assist the U.S perform her imperialist action in Chad.

This move which was far beyond the capacity of the Nigerian army logistically and in terms of securing and maintaining proper understanding of the factions-was a huge disaster. The Shagari government was accused of serving as mercenary nation "to protect the U.S interest".[19] In fact, Colonel Magoro, who led the operation described the peacekeeping operation as a "hasty entry and withdrawal"[20] which is devoid of rigorous preparation on the part of Nigerian troops. He added that there was "lack of proper briefing on the factional leaders and their factions"[21] as well as lack of legal instrument spelling out the status of Nigerian troops.

Bolaji Akinyemi, former foreign minister under Babangida, was also of the view that the peace-keeping force in Chad was a failure because:

> It was hastily conceived and it was ill conceived. There was no status-of-forces agreement with the Chadians, the troops were not briefed as to their mission and those sending then did not have the correct perception of what a peace-keeping mission was all about... the Nigerian peace-keeping Mission lacked.[22]

In Bus therefore, what these episodes demonstrate is the limitation of Nigeria's power to undertake effective and credible joint or literal peace-keeping operation which points to the fact that Nigeria had no dynamic foreign policy posture under the Shagari government.

NIGERIA-CAMEROON

The border skirmishes between Nigeria and Cameroon in 1981 was another instance in which the Shagari administration failed to stop the harassment of Nigerian villagers and fishermen along the country's borders and this to a considerable extent exposed the unreliable and fragile basis of Nigeria's foreign policy in the second Republic. All the Shagari administration could do at best, was to appeal to the OAU to bring Cameroon into line.

Though internal opinion was divided, there were calls for either an invasion of Cameroon or the use of the army to recapture Nigerian villages from the Cameroonians. After tracing the ineptitude of the Shagari government in dealing with the neighboring countries, The *Guardian* criticized the government in an editorial entitled: "Cameroon has to be stopped" in which it accused the government of failing to protect the interests of the country. Generally, because of the diplomatic rudeness or lack of normative rule displayed by the Cameroonian government Bending a very junior minister to Nigeria on the issue.

Furthermore, some Nigerians were of the opinion that it was necessary to " test its soldiers" externally and teach Cameroon a lesson. It was possible at that time that the recourse to the OAU over the border clashes was rational, but more importantly, the Shagari administration was scared by the politicization of the issues at home. Also, the wide level of public dissatisfaction with the government conditioned the Nigerian response to border clashes. These unfavorable internal conditions highlighted above, militated against the idea of resolving the Cameroonian issue through war. These and other internal conditions bedeviled the foreign policy pastures of Nigeria between 1979 and 1983.

NIGERIA AND ISRAEL

The Shagari government decision of 1981 to allow the Palestinian Liberation Organization (PLO) to open an office in Lagos by early April 1985 has not been favored by the military rulers, instead, have hardened their attitudes to Israel.[23] While few African states such as Kenya, Ivory Coast, and Ghana under Rawlings opened channels of communications with Israel, since 1983 by allowing it to open information offices on their territories, the Shagari government blocked such official communication with the state of Israel long after the Camp David Accord had been signed.

The issue of resumption of diplomatic ties with Israel has, however, generated a lot of controversies, reaction from the articulate Nigerians. While the predominantly Christians in the South and their vocal press such as the *Daily Sketch, The Nigeria Tribune; The Guardian* have advocated a resumption of diplomatic ties with Israel, the largely predominant Muslim population of the North ably supported by the "*New Nigerian*" group of newspaper campaigned for tougher policies against Israel.

It is significant to note that the severing of diplomatic relations with Israel on the basis of its (Israel's) relations with South Africa should have been made to cover all nations having relations with South Africa. Again, the government claimed to have no diplomatic relationship with Israel, but Israeli firms were not only in the construction and oil sectors, but they also won government contracts. Failure to re-open diplomatic relations with Israel can then be attributed to facts such as:

(I) The Islamic region to which the president subscribe to, coupled with the powerful influence of pro-Arab and pro-Islamic lobby of the Northern aristocrats,
(II) The desire to maintain the radical stance of the military regime,
(III)The urge to retain Nigeria's claim of leadership and initiation in the continent.[24]

Alhaji Shehu Shagari made a categorical statements on the Middle East situation in July 1981 when he expressed Nigeria's continuing concern for peace and justice in the middle east, particularly with reference to the inalienable rights of the Palestinians to self determination and a national home. The president rightly declared:

> Nigeria condemns without preservation Israel's continuing occupation of Palestinians and other Arab territories... We cannot support any decision or act on the part of Israel to change the status of the old Jerusalem. Nor shall we accept any unilateral action by Israel to alter the character of the occupied Arab territories by planning Jewish settlement in them.[25]

The president have on several other international occasions, restated his administration stand on the Middle East question. For he maintained that the Palestinian issue was extremely important and serious which requires urgent solution. He believed that the Palestinians deserved to have their own homeland returned to them.

However, with the absence of a concrete link between Nigeria and Israel, the Palestinian issue was dropped just like other pressing issues due to lack of sanction.

NIGERIA AND THE OAU

The inability of Shagari's administration to command respect of other African (especially ECOWAS) states on issues concerning the continent, more importantly, in her failure in the Chadian crisis test stemmed from three interwoven factors.

Firstly, Nigeria could not serve as the alternative to the Western donor countries. Nigeria's performance during the Chadians crisis and the Nigerian ameroon border clashes have gone a long way to prove that Nigeria cannot be relied upon in times of emergency.

Secondly, one would notice that during the Shagari's administration there was economic crisis in the country. The ruling faction of the Nigerian bourgeoisie were reactionary conservative in nature, hence its inability to maintain the extravagant and false posture inherited from the military.

Furthermore, Nigeria was for more dependence on Western powers and as such when issues involved these powers, Nigeria had to tear down its aggressiveness. That accounted Shagari's government failure to condemn the United States invasion of Granada later in October 1983, which was violently attacked in a fiery editorial entitled "Big for Notting".

Finally, Nigeria foreign policy in the Second Republic hardly lived up to the standards set by the military. Indeed, it was escapist and diversionary. Real issues were avoided and broad utopian goals were pursued.

A columnist, Emmanuel Yawe, in a piece in *Sunday New Nigerian* accused Shagari adminisration of reversing "the minimal achievement in foreign policy of the military administration, and shot back to the early years of independence when Nigeria was unable to take any stand on any international issue without consulting the West.[26] The failure of his administration to recognize the POLISARIO government, the Saharawi Arab Democratic Republic (SADR) could readily be understood.

Shortly after the military putsch there were many criticism of the Shagari foreign policy. General Mohammed Buhari in his maiden address to the nation said "inter alia" in an implicit condemnation of the previous foreign policy that his government would pursue "a dynamic and realistic foreign policy."[27]

General, T.Y. Danjuna, the Chief Army Staff from 1975 until October 1979 said late in January 1984 that under the Shagari administration Nigeria "lost her voice and position of influence in international affairs"[28]. Indeed, the point remains that Nigeria has failed to lend its weight if at all she ever has one in support of the Organization of African Unity(OAU) in the latter's attempt to end the excess dependence on the opponents of the OAU and the African continents - namely the metropolitan countries of Europe and America.

Major General Joe Garba, the then Nigerian permanent Representative at the United Nations, said shortly after the military take over that Nigeria foreign policy was dangerous and too subservient to the United States.[29]

CONCLUSION

Projecting into any country's future is generally a dangerous assignment. In Nigeria's case, one can almost be certain that events are not static but ever changing. Perhaps the only thing that we can postulate with some degree of certainty is that the next ten years for Nigeria will be critical ones - especially for her domestic position, its role in Africa and the International Community. However, since charity begins at home, any country's foreign policy, as well known, is a function of its internal politics and economy. The availability of oil revenue in the 70's had a considerable impact on Nigeria's foreign policy options. As shown in the chapter, one of the reasons that have been responsible for overthrow of regimes in Nigeria have however, been the lack of commitment to civil duties. Yakubu Gowon was overthrown in 1975 because he went back on his 1976 deadline for the return to civil rule. The Murtala/Obasanio regime took over power, came in with a promise of returning the country back to civil rule. This commitment remained and was later translated into handing over to President Shehu Shagari in October 1979.

The Shagari administration as the governing arm of local bourgeoisie, conveniently overlooked how substructural (internal) contradictions and relations of production and capital accumulation combined to influence policies towards outside world. The December 1983 military take over occurred as a result of endemic forces that were largely internal - misrule, mismanagement of the economy, endemic political violence, instability and insecurity arising from the rigged elections of August/ September 1983 as well unparalleled corruption in public life. And the dismal failure to address internal problems reflected at the international level.

The maiden address of General Buhari on January 1, 1984, centered on how to rescue Nigerians and the world at large on the future of Nigeria's foreign policy. He said that the federal military government would maintain and strengthen diplomatic relations with other states and with international organizations, will honor and respect all treaty obligations entered into by the previous governments. Within matter of months, the regime had lost the goodwill of the Nigerian public for a number of reasons. One of the reasons can be attributed to the systematic manner it went about destroying the fabrics of certain power groups - the press, labor, students and professionals.

Although the governments closure of the borders for almost 15 months and the expulsion of some so called "illegal immigrants" on economic ground was inconsistent with Nigeria's objective of promoting sub-regionalism. The regime, however, injected new life into old policies by actively supporting liberation movements and fashioning a policy which focused on national security, economic well-being and the famous concentric circle theory.

The Babangida regime came in August 1985, with a promise of popular participation in government, through public debates, recognition and acceptance of the role and importance of certain civilian power groups, a greater commitment to respect fundamental human rights and return of the country to civil rule.[30] Babangida regime, was regarded as an offshoot of the Buhari regime and, therefore, unlikely to divert significantly on main thrust of that regimes foreign Policy. However, the economics problems of the Country imposed some limitations and compel both a new approach and a new focus in Nigeria foreign policy. Thus, the management of international economic Relations became the most important assignment of Babangida foreign policy. This manifested itself in the series of national debate on the IMF loan and diplomatic shuttle to western capitals - London and Paris, known as "Economic Diplomacy".

On recurrent political issues, however, the Babangida regime has been concerned with ensuring that relations are not impaired by the methods employed in their dealings and impact of the image presented. These have featured official actions and pronouncements. It is anticipated, however, that in spite of the legacy of the Nigerian past, emerging international issues, particularly issues concerning Nigeria and neighboring states, coupled with committed and dedicated leaders could make Nigerian leaders' face new realities and courses of actions beneficial to Nigeria in her foreign policy options.

Whatever the rhetoric and realities, the military leaders have not undertaken or developed any radical approach since Alhaji Shehu Shagari regime to show some changes in the direction of Nigeria's foreign policy, the fact remains that the sub-structural dimension has remained constant. Although the power show under Abacha has shown the potential of Nigeria's ability within the region - its actions in Liberia and Sierra Leone is extremely interesting considering that the military continue to rule in Nigeria, while she attempts to instill democracy in another.

Given that he military inherited a badly managed economy, the socioeconomic policies embarked upon have hardly addressed the issue of popular mobilization, self-reliance and collective involvement in the process of national development to build a credible and viable base for the country's external relations. This is not to say that there has not been major development in Nigeria's external relations since the Second Republic. The difference the military has made seem to relate to the level of commitment and degree of vigor of pursuing these policies.

Amongst the areas where the military regime had intensified effort were, the hosting of ECOWAS and Medium Range powers Summits at Abuja and Lagos respectively and playing an important role in the ECOMOG and the resolution of conflict and peace-making in Liberia. Earlier on, we also have retired Generals Obasanjo and Gowon's participation in the Eminent Persons Group of Commonwealth and ECOWAS countries respectively. The issue of I.M.F. and the Organization of Islamic Conference, and the institution of Transitional program and democratic dispensation that was aimed originally to terminate in 1990, then 1993, the annulment of June 13 1993 election, the transitional government of Shonekan and its removal by Abacha all have dominated Nigeria's political landscape and creating a reactive and isolated policy in light of the killing of Ken Sarowiwa, the imprisonment of civil right activists.

General Babangida as OAU Chairman successfully plotted the strategy that culminated in the election of an African as UN Secretary - General. Attraction of support of leading financial institutions through "economic diplomacy" for implementation of Structural Adjustment Program (SAP), and the promotion and maintenance of regional peace and security by spearheading the formation of Economic Community of West African Monitoring Group (ECO"OG). More importantly, was General Babangida's address to the 46th Session of the United Nations General Assembly on the 4th of October 1991 on Africa's expectation from the emerging new world order.

His speech championed the course of the poor majority which received an open ovation and ended by calling for the expansion of the Security Council to include additional permanent members and making good case for an African to succeed Perez De Cueller as Secretary - General[31]

These developments have generated a lot of debates at home and abroad, but have all been influenced by the nature of military leadership and decision making process, mass poverty and tensions at home and the fragility of the state hegemony.

In the new Third Republic, Nigeria to become the real giant, must be able to maximize its potentials by effectively tapping her domestic resources and increase the local content of finished products. In a related development, the federal military government have started the compilation of the first ever directory of Scientists in the country. In addition, the government have also made contacts with International Organizations and have instituted the necessary machinery to establish Science and Technology Attaché in Nigerian Embassies. These attempts and others will lead to another "gold mine" of scientific and technological potentials of Nigeria.[32]

Furthermore, on trade issues, if wise counsel prevails and Africa wants to move toward economic integration and avoid its present marginalization, Nigeria and South Africa could work in harmony to mobilize a technological revolution in Africa[33]. Most importantly, by pooling their advantages - Nigeria's formidable range of natural resources - oil and gas reserves together with South Africa's "first world" technological base. These two countries could at last break the pattern of dependence that has bedeviled Africa.

Though the possibility of such an alliance between Nigeria and South Africa makes a number of reasonable probabilities. Firstly, that the present trade regime in Africa has to be radically changed. Attention will however, have to be made towards promoting intra-African trade, and bigger economies like Nigeria and South Africa will have to address the legitimate fears expressed by smaller states. Nigeria will have a particularly important role in fostering economic integration. Its position in ensuring that the smallest member state of ECOWAS benefit will serve as an example.

South Africa will have to be similarly judicious if it is accepted into the Southern African Coordinating Conference (SADCC). Also noticeable was the fact that the holding of such conferences, such as the All Nigerian Foreign policy held in Kuru, JOB, was a commendable effort. The inability of the press to raise debate and encourage discussion of foreign policy option for the new Republic could be more than a product of the relationship between the government and the press in Nigeria. The few criticisms, however, Suggests that newspapers had a certain leverage in the coverage of foreign policy issues.

Increasing Nigeria's political and economic clout on the international scene will of course depend on its internal affairs. There must be a successful return to civil rule. Various machinery set up by President Babangida to "civilianize" the government have undergone series of changes. The Abacha regime which in itself, is an off-shoot of that administration has continue the process but the fear, is the incessant military intervention which continue to undermine socio-political and economic development. However, there are those opposed to the handover on the grounds that the Third Republic will merely be a rerun of the ill fated Second Republic. Unfortunately, this argument holds weight - there is a strong element of "money politics" in Nigeria. The banning of the old politicians had not succeeded in purging Nigeria's body politic. Nor has the system of government sponsored political parties - the National Republican Convention (NRC), and the Social Democratic Party (SDP) with their near identical manifestos.

It must be emphasized, however, that the key ingredient for the success of the new political order will be accountability and economic growth. Nigeria's political credibility question comes again into play. The thought use to be that if Nigeria can organize an orderly and fair transition to civil rule through free and fair elections, it will give South Africa and other Nations in the continent moral support in their bid for a constitutional revolution but the reverse is the case, because democratic transition and sustainable constitutional government in other African states, especially South Africa is an inspiration for Nigeria. On the other hand, if the Nigerian enterprise descend further into chaos, it will have repercussions across Africa.

Notes

1) Guardian (Lagos) 10 January, 1986.
2) Nigerians have made no secret of their refusal to accept Dr. Nkrumah as a messiah in African politics. For more details, Bee Editorial, The West African Pilot (Lagos) 13 October, 1960.
3) For details of these statements, see House of Representatives Debates, August 1960 Session, pp.289-290. Bee also Sanjiva Nayak "Foundation of the Foreign Policy of Nigeria" Africa Quarterly, New Delhi, Vol.2, 1962. pp. 118-128.
4) Ibrahim Gambari "Nigerian Foreign Policy at the Crossroads: Concepts, Critical Issues and Management of External Relations under the Buhari Administration" in A.B. Akinyeni et. al (eds) Nigeria Since Independence-The First 25 Years. (Nigeria: Heinemann Educational Books Ltd, 1989).p.275.
5) See B. Freund, "Oil Boom and Crisis in Contemporary Nigeria", Review of African Political Economy 13, 1979.

6) For more details, Bee "A Win for Africa" West Africa Nov 30, 1987. pp. 2332-4. See also Amechi Okolo, "Nigeria and the Superpowers" in A.B. Akinyeni et.al (ed) op.cit. pp.65-66.
7) The Constitution of the Federal Republic of Nigeria, 1979 (Lagos: Government Printer, 1979) Paragraph 19.
8) Ibid. Section. 122.
9) Ibid., Section 12.
10) Ibid., Section 5, Sub-section 3.
11) For more details on Party primaries rumpus, See West Africa, II - 17 Nov. 1991. p.1680.
12) See " Ensuring a Successful Transition" West Africa, 11-17 Nov.1991.
13) For more detailed analysis of the five political parties, Bee I.W.Zartman (ed) The Political Economy of Nigeria (New York: Praeger Publishers, 1983).
14) T. Falola and J.Ihonvbere, The Rise and Fall of Nigeria's Second Republic, 1979-84. (London:Zed Press 1985) Chapter V. See also J.O. Ihonvbere, "Oil Revenues, Rural-Urban Inequalities in Nigeria". Paper presented to the International Conference Organised by the Institute of International Co-operation and Development, University of Ottawa, October, 1981.
15) Daily Times (Lagos) May 8, 1984.
16) Daily Times (Lagos) May 9, 1984. For further details, See Central Bank of Nigeria (CBN), Annual Reports and Statement of Accounts, 1979.
17) The Guardian (Lagos) Nov. 5, 1983.
18) O. Aluko. Nigerian Foreign Policy under the Second Republic. Address to the Foreign Service Academy, Lagos: Dec. 1964.
19) Sunday Punch, (Lagos) Dec.11, 1983.
20) For details, see Colonel M. Magoro, "Nigeria's Peace - Keeping Role in Chad", Lagos: Nigerian Institute of International Affairs, n.d.
21) Ibid.
22) A.B. Akinyesi, "Chad: The Lesson for Nigeria", Nigerian Forum Lagos: N.I.I.A., March 1, 1981. p.8. 23. The tough measures taken against two traditional rulers - Ooni of Ife, and the Emir of Kano - that visited Israel late in 1984 was a testimony to this hardening of attitude to the Israelis.
24) A.Adigun, "Economy and Foreign Policy: A Case Study of Nigeria's Second Republic (1979-1983)". Unpublished B.Sc. Long Essay, Department of International Relations, Obafemi Awolowo University, Ile-Ife, Nigeria, June 1986. p.74.

25) See Shehu Shagari, Address to Summit Conference of OAU in Freetown, Sierra Leone, July 1980.
26) Sunday New Nigerian (Kaduna), Feb. 19, 1984.
27) Daily Times (Lagos), Jan. 2, 1984.
28) O.Aluko. op.cit. p.3.
29) New Nigerian (Kaduna), Jan. 27, 1984.
30) See Ade Adefuye. "The Commonwealth and Nigeria in a New World Order". Text presented at the first Olasupo Ojedokun Memorial Lectures held at the Nigerian Institute of International Affairs, Lagos, April 24, 1992.
31) See the authors work "Indigenous Technology and Industrialization in Developing Countries: A Case Study of Nigeria", Science, Technology and Development. Journal of Third World Science, Vol.9, Nos.1 & 2, April/ August, 1991. p.216. Also see Aderemi Ajibewa "Regional Security Problems and Needs" Quarterly Journal of Administration Nos I & 2, Vol XXIV October 1989/January, 1990. pp 82-92.
32) For more details, see the authors work "The International Dimension of Perestroika and Glasnost: Challenge of changes in Eastern Europe for Africa". Paper presented at the Annual Conference of Development Studies Association, University of Glasgow, 5-7 Sept, 1991.

Chapter Six

MANAGING NIGERIA'S MARKETING SYSTEM IN THE THIRD REPUBLIC

Philemon O. Oyewole

1. INTRODUCTION

Going by the definition of the American Marketing Association, MARKETING is "the process of planning and executing the conception, pricing, promotion, and distribution of ideas, goods, and services to create exchanges that satisfy individual and organizational objectives" (A.M.A., 1983 p.1).

The part of this definition that interests us most is "planning and executing". Whereas the functions of conception, pricing, promotion and distribution of ideas, goods, services are being performed, one way or the other, in the Nigeria's economy, they can hardly be said to be well planned and effectively executed. The lack of planning and effective execution of these important functions in the economy betrays the neglect of marketing as a managerial function by the successive powers that be (Odia, 1979).

This neglect is to be regretted as marketing has been shown to play important roles in the development of industrialized nations, and in the economic success of newly industrializing nations like South Korea. Empirical studies reported that merchants have made the leading contributions to early industrialization in such countries as Pakistan, Greece, Turkey, and the Philippines (see Papenek, 1962, Alexander, 1960, and Alexander, 1968).

As Nwokoye (1981), pointed out, marketing contributes to the economic progress of a country in the following ways, among others:

(i) by extending markets for goods and services resulting in promotion of specialization and of production for sale;
(ii) by stimulating the accumulation of capital needed for industrialization; and
(iii) by creating a merchant class which in turn becomes a major source of entrepreneurial and managerial talent needed to establish and run manufacturing enterprises.

It can be argued that China, India, Indonesia, and Thailand have been successful in stimulating food production by relying on marketing and market forces. Likewise, the success in South east Asia on the economic, political, and social fronts can be attributed to the role of marketing in distribution, information dissemination, education and so forth (Hosley and Hou wee, 1988).

In her search for viable alternatives to economic recovery in the third republic, Nigeria cannot afford to continue to neglect marketing. It is imperative to design a well planned marketing system throughout the federation, and set up a structure for the effective management of the system. Suggestions towards this goal are given in this chapter, which is divided into 6 sections.

After this section 1 on introduction, section 2 will review the literature on the role of marketing in economic development. Section 3 describes the present structure and functioning of marketing in the country, while section 4 analyze the inefficiencies in the system. Section 5 suggests a marketing system for the third republic, and outlines a program for its effective management. Section 6 resumes and concludes the chapter.

2 The Role of Marketing in Economic Development

A review of the literature reveals two schools of thought, among scholars, on the relationship of marketing with national development. We have the determinist and the activists (Hilger, 1978; Duhaime et al, 1985). The determinist argue that marketing only responds to the national environment playing only a passive role in development. In one word, the level of development determines the level of sophistication of the marketing system. The activists, on the other hand, argue that marketing influences the national environment and plays an active role in development. They view marketing as leading development.

2.1 Determinist Theory

According to the determinist school of thought, the roles, functions, and systems of marketing are dictated by such characteristics of the society as the size and density of the population, the size of the area served, the transportation and communication infrastructures, the volume and variety of goods produced, as well as, the human factors such as the level of literacy, customs and traditions of the populace. Marketing is said to adapt to environmental changes, and marketing performance indicators are seen as closely related to levels of economic development.

Expressing a determinist point of view, Baker (1969) stated that the Nigerian collective markets remain at the heart of the economy representing "an effective adaptation of the needs and facilities of the people to the environmental setting of the land", which setting includes a hot, humid climate, a profusion of edible products, a high population density and low purchasing power.

Moyer (1968), expressed the viewpoint that as an economy develops, its marketing organizations automatically develop as well. Thus, from the barter stage, where the producer is also the distributor, an expanded market emerges with full-time intermediaries, as is the case in most economies today. Arndt (1972) in his own case reported haven found retail performance depending on such factors as population concentration, the GDP, and consumption per capita. Hansz and Goodnow (1973) also reported a relationship between market performance and such variables as television sets, newspapers per capita, and road density.

Preston (1968), from a study of 79 countries at different levels of development concluded that the ratio of tertiary employment to total employment is a function of the level of economic development in the countries studied. Currie (1968) arrived at similar conclusion in his study of the effect of social and cultural conditions on large scale marketing and retailing institutions in Africa.

In their critique of the determinist theory, Hosley and Hou Wee (1988 p.47) said, among other things, that "the determinist school appeals more in the sphere of international rather than domestic marketing. For the former, adaptation is necessary to survive. For the latter, it may be crucial to control and hence chart events in order to ensure balanced growth within a country". This view is strongly supported by the present writer.

2.2 Activist Theory

Peter Drucker (1958), though not regarded as an activist himself, was the first to express an activist view of marketing saying, among other things, that marketing, much more than manufacturing or construction, is the most important "multiplier" of development. He sees in marketing the greatest challenge, and greatest potential payback to developing societies. The first "activist" was Walt Rostow (1965), who submitted that the most important factor for further economic growth in an underdeveloped national economy was the development of a national market system.

Alexander (1968), from his studies of Turkey, Pakistan, Greece and the Philippines that it was the merchants with their entrepreneurial ability and capital, accumulated from trading activities, who became the original industrialists in these countries. Glade and Udell (1968) and Slater (1968), all activists, advocated the improvement of distribution systems as a means of stimulating economic development. Miracle (1968), studied West African market places, and suggested that increased competition in distribution would increase not only channel efficiency but also the rate of capital accumulation of peasants thereby raising their productivity.

Layton (1981), from his work on central Java, concluded that such things as innovation in channel structure can have a pivotal role in altering income per capita. Anderson (1970), studied Thailand and concluded that storage facilities and food processing activities are factors that contribute to more efficient distribution channel and thus economic development. Cundiff and Hilger (1979) have expressed the believe that the transfer of marketing techniques and know-how to managers in developing countries would stimulate development. Cundiff (1982), added that, "a necessary step is the development of a corps of local managers competent to use modern marketing technology. First, this involves changing the generally negative image of business, as compared with the professions, that exists in most underdeveloped countries" (p.17).

In summary the activist theory teaches that economic development results from correct modification of the components of the marketing infrastructure, such as, transportation and storage facilities, credit and banking facilities, as well as, creation of marketing institutions and dissemination of information both in the form of consumer and market research data (Hosley and Hou Wee, 1988, p.47). Before concluding this section of literature review on the role of marketing in economic development, it should be pointed out that a few scholars have expressed the view that marketing both stimulates development and responds to it. Nwokoye (1981) stated that "Marketing provides the driving force for economic development, and the level of economic activity in turn affects the sophistication of the marketing system"(p.7). Kinsey (1982), also expressed the view that, "Marketing acts both as a catalyst for economic development and as a response to it"; He goes on to say that, "It is often difficult to distinguish whether marketing plays a "leading" or a "lagging" role. It is suggested here that it can play either, and in some economies it has played, or is playing both. *If rapid economic is development induced, marketing can prove a highly useful tool.* If economic development occurs spontaneously, marketing will lag behind until a certain point is reached" (p.68, italics is authors).

The writer is of the view that what Nigeria needs, in the 3rd Republic, is an "induced" economic development, and as Kinsey stated, marketing can prove a highly useful tool.

3 Structure and Functioning of the Nigerian Marketing System

Present Nigerian marketing system can be said to be two-structured. On the one hand, we have the modern supermarket system with store layouts closely following the patterns in the industrialized nations. On the other hand, we have the traditional market system, with a large number of market men and women selling their wares individually in rotating markets of a four - five-, or seven-day cycle, drawing from a radius of 10 - 25 miles. These individual stall operators can also be found stationed along street corners, and bus stops, at motor garages and outside railway stations and airports. There are also a good number of these individual traders hawking their wares freely on the streets, and even on the motor ways, taking advantage of the unending go-slows in the big cities.

The supermarkets are usually found in the big cities only. They are usually owned by big expatriate trading firms such as United African Company (U.A.C.), Union Trading Company (U.T.C.), Kaycee, Leventis Stores Limited, Kingsway Stores Limited, and Chellarams Stores Limited. These supermarkets cater primarily to the upper class (which is very limited), while the lower class (the majority) frequent the more traditional markets. Apart from the accessibility factor (the supermarkets are usually located in the busy centers of big cities), there is also important price differential between goods sold in the local markets and those sold in the supermarkets.

The supermarkets, for the most part, have centralized purchasing and pricing systems resulting in the branch manager performing little or no marketing functions. All decisions are made in the head office. Very few, advertising and sales promotion are done. Most of the times, these big trading company limit their advertising to sponsoring diffusion of sports and matches on the television. Marketing research are hardly undertaken by these supermarkets. This function is left to the care of manufacturing firms like Lever Brothers(Nigeria) Ltd., Nestles, and the firms in the brewery industry. However, the market research carried out by these manufacturing firms are often in the form of feasibility studies for new enterprises (Nnolim, 1979). These firms do invest on advertising their individual products but they are not able to control their distribution channel, as the supermarkets, and the market men and women operate independently.

The traditional market system provides the main outlet for agricultural products especially food items. The importance of this market system is easily appreciated when one realizes that between half to three quarters of the income of the entire inhabitants of the country is spent on food, as is the case in most developing nations (F.A.O., 1976). The operators of the traditional market system are the individual market men and women. Each one decides on what to sell, how, when, and even where to sell. Advertising is not done in the modern sense of the term. Individual trader call attention to his/her wares by shouting out, at a loud voice, the supposed good qualities of each items for sale, or by ringing a bell continuously to attract by passers and shoppers.

While prices are fixed at the corporate offices for the supermarkets, the haggling system is adopted in the traditional market. This system is schematized in Figures 1, 2, and 3.

Briefly, the haggling system operates as follows: no price is marked on the product for sale, unlike is done in the supermarkets. The potential buyer asks for

Figure 1: A Structure for the Nigeria's Economic System in the Third Republic

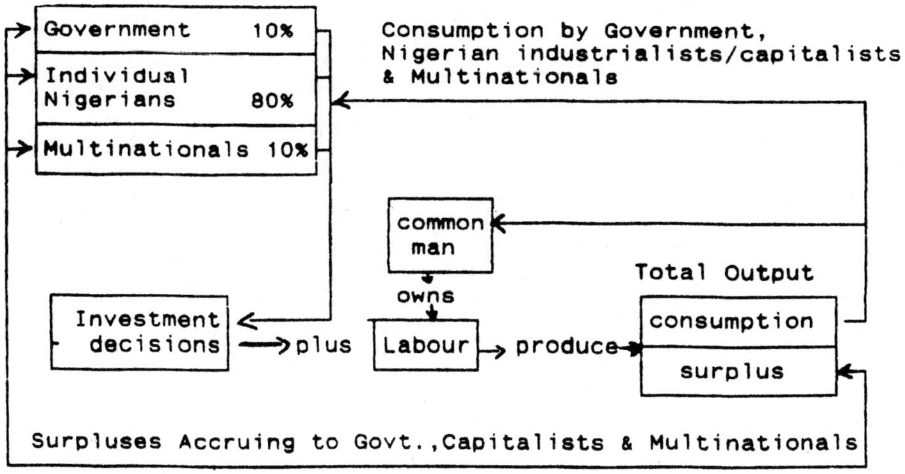

In the above figure, a greater percentage of investment decisions are made by Nigerians operating as individuals or as corporate bodies.

Figure 2: The Role of Government in the Nigerian's Industrial Relations in the Third World Republic.

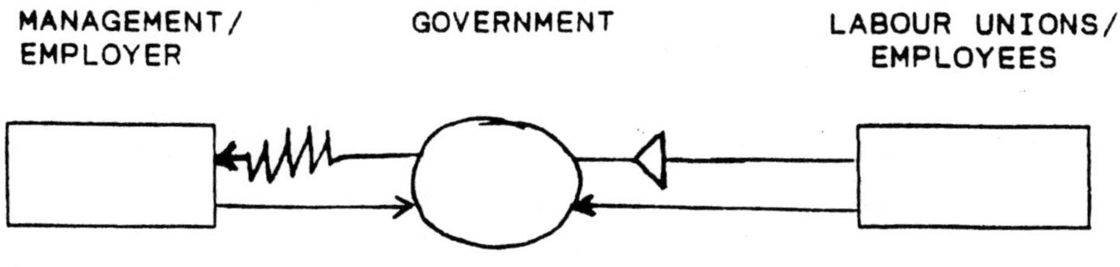

Figure 3: The System of Haggling

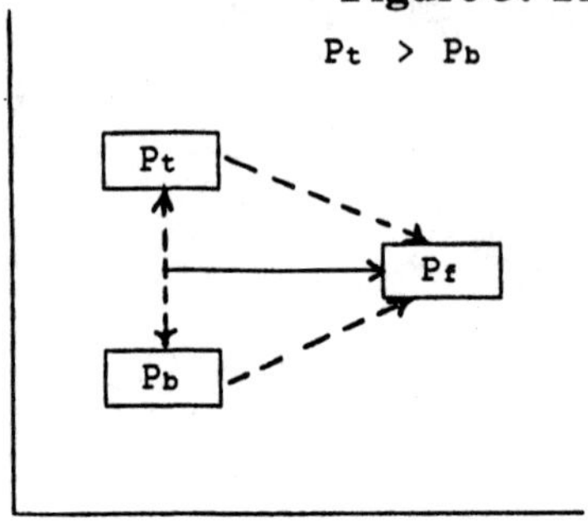

FIG. 1

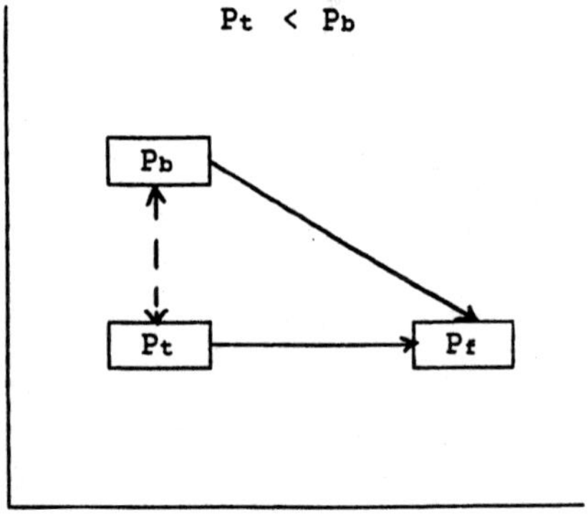

FIG.2

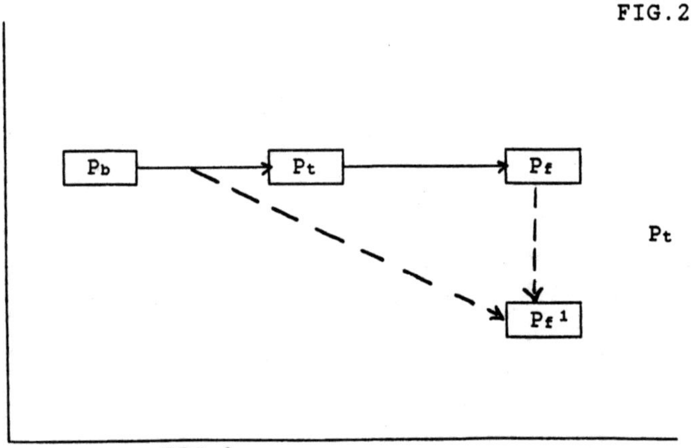

FIG.3

Key:

P_t = Trader's price; P_b = Buyer's price; P_f and $P_f{}^1$= Probable final price;

the price of the item s/he is interested in. The trader announces a price which is generally higher than the final price acceptable. Of course, the buyer himself/herself has got a personal reference price which s/he considers the right price for the item. If the price announced by the trader, (Pt), is higher than the buyer's reference price, (Pt), as in Fig.1, the buyer negotiate with the trader to lower the price. After a certain time, the two agree on a price **Pf,** which is usually lower than Pt, but may be equal to, or higher a bit than, than **Pb.**

On the other hand, if Pt is lower than Pb, as in Fig. 2, the buyer is generally ready to buy at price **Pt** without any prolonged negotiation. In this case the **Pf** is equal to **Pt.**

Finally, if Pt is equal to Pb, as in Fig. 3, often the buyer attempts to lower the price further by negotiating. The final price accepted may then be equal to, or lower than both Pt and **Pb.**

It is an acceptable practice than one should negotiate, for a lower price, when buying under the traditional marketing system, even if one is buying only a piece of yam.

Like their supermarket counterpart, no market research is undertaken in the traditional market system. If there is anything that the traditional market system does better than the supermarket system, it is in the domain of product accessibility to the consumer. The traders, or operators of the traditional market system are found all over the country, rural and urban areas alike, transporting their wares on foot to every nook and corner of the town or city. Practically, they bring the market to the consumers doorsteps, or car steps, as the case may be.

While the supermarkets specialize in selling at retail level, the operators of the traditional market system sell both at retail, and wholesale levels. Some of these operators classify themselves as wholesalers, but the irony is that they are ready to sell also on retail at any time, if a buyer so wish. In addition, we still have some small scale farmers who bring their produce personally to the main roads and nearby markets for sale, thus acting as both producer and seller. This is one of the reasons why Nnolim (1979, p.11) says that " marketing institutions and functions are still in the developing stage in Nigeria...... The internal distribution of most agricultural commodities is disorganized to the point of being chaotic." In the next section, we examine some of the major inefficiencies in the current marketing system, after which, a suggested line of actions will be given to alleviate them in the 3rd republic.

4 Inefficiencies in the Current Marketing System

The traditional marketing system, as operated currently in the country, is fraught with many inefficiencies, thus denying the nation the contribution marketing could have made to her economic development.

Firstly, the large number of individual petty traders, illiterate for the most part, find it hard to coordinate their efforts resulting in different standards of services rendered to the consumer for similar prices. Sometimes, it is difficult to distinguish wholesalers from retailers, as the wholesalers also sell on retail. The benefits of specialization is thus lost to the traders and consumers alike.

Further, the traditional marketing system is labor intensive, leading to undue increases in the prices paid by the consumer. The operators of the system lack the knowledge, or the fund, or both to make use of modern storage facilities such as refrigerated warehouses, nor to invest on large scale warehouses, processing plants and trucks to cut down cost of storage, processing, and transportation. A reason for this lack of knowledge, and fund may be found in the fact that most traders start commercial activities too young, and thus, ill prepared for all it takes to be a successful and productive middleman. Often people see in commercial activities an employment of last resort when efforts in all other sectors of the economy have failed. The view is that trading needs little, or no training and only a few is needed to start. This erroneous view is evidenced in under aged boys and girls found engaged in commercial activities. Young ones who should still be at primary school are already on the streets selling as professional traders.

Street hawking is a common feature of the traditional marketing system. Apart from being an eyesore in any 20th century country, the practice is a source of inefficiencies, and can hardly make any appreciable positive contributions to economic development. The practice over-utilizes labor and is tiring to the street peddler who often carries his/her wares on the head, and go several kilometers on foot soliciting for buyers. The street peddler is not encouraged to expand his/her business and enjoy the benefits of scale, as s/he can afford to carry about only such weight that his or her power can bear. A lot of time is wasted going about the street with the result that a whole day is spent selling only a few articles. Given the huge number of street peddlers found all over the country, one can only appreciate the amount of man-hours lost to the economy by this practice.

The situation in the traditional marketplaces also give rise to certain inefficiencies. These market places are often poorly designed. The environment is hardly hygienic and public utilities are exceptions rather than the rule. Often pipe borne water is not available. Especially food items, in such environment, present dangers to human health. Precious man-hours are lost, curing an avoidable sickness, instead of engaging in useful economic activities. As the market stalls are not equipped with modern storage facilities, physical losses due to dehydration, pests, and diseases are high. The layout of the market places is often confusing and there are no signboards or posters indicating where specific articles are sold. A shopper may need to walk the length and breadth of a market place and search all its nooks, and corners before s/he can get all s/he wants to buy.

This leads to a considerable waste of man-hours that could better be used in other more productive economic activities.

The system of haggling, employed in the traditional marketing system to arrive at a price is a most inefficient method. As could be seen from the description of the system given above, a lot of time is spent arriving at a price for each item to be purchased and sold. This represent a waste of time to the seller who could have attended to more clients, to the shopper who could have done more purchases in lesser time, and to the national economy that loses precious man-hours. The system of haggling also gives room for non-uniform prices for the same product and service in the same locality. Prices paid and received depend upon the level of one's skill at haggling. Consequently, two different shoppers may pay two different prices for the same product or service purchased from the same person. This is rather unfair to the consuming public and does not encourage a good consumer/seller relationship.

The system of haggling also prevent the trader from working out his/her profit margin in advance, as he or she is not sure of the final selling price. Under this situation, volume expansion is not encouraged as no positive relation could be established between volume of sale and marginal profit. The result is that a huge number of petty traders remain petty.

While the supermarket system may be better organized than the traditional marketing system, it is not without some inefficiencies. The spatial distribution of the supermarkets does not does not permit the inhabitants of the small towns and villages to benefit from their services. In addition, the supermarkets do not furnish needed market information to either the producers, or the consumers as they rarely carry out any market research.

Added to all the inefficiencies, discussed above, are the infrastructural inefficiencies, such as, lack of good roads, pipe borne water, and regular supply of electricity. With lack of adequate transportation facilities, from the farm to the market place, the peasant farmer produces only enough for his consumption, with only a little addition that could be carried to the market on the head. The economies of scale are thus denied the farmer and, indirectly the national economy as well.

In the face of all these inefficiencies, a better management of the marketing system in the country is urgently called for. Suggestions towards this end are now given in the following section.

5 Suggestions for a Better Management of the Marketing System in the Third Republic

Before talking of "managing" we deem it fit to first talk of "what" is to be managed. The present marketing system in the country is "chaotic", and thus difficult to manage. This is especially true of the traditional marketing system, as discussed above. This system however, is the dominant system in the economy, and its inefficiencies overshadow any efficiency that could be attributed to the supermarket system. If then we could borrow from the idea of the "activist", Walt Rostow (1965), who stated that the most important factor for further economic growth in an underdeveloped national economy is the development of a national market system, an alternative system to the present traditional marketing system must be found.

An overnight eradication of the traditional marketing system, replaced by the modern marketing system as is practiced in the developed countries will an impossible mission in the 3rd republic. The present level of technology in the country, as well as the social-cultural factors of the environment may not be able to support such project as at present. Such a goal is best reserved for a more distant future. For the immediate future, a restructuring of the traditional marketing system is both feasible, and plausible. We thus suggest, for the 3rd Republic, a system that we term MODERNIZED TRADITIONAL MARKETING SYSTEM. The structure and functioning of this system are detailed below.

5.1 Modernised Traditional Marketing System

The actors in the modernized traditional marketing system will include the local manufacturers, the private farmers, the government agricultural farms, and the importers - acting as suppliers; the processing wholesalers, the distributing wholesalers, the retailers, the supermarkets, and the consumer cooperative societies - acting as marketers; and finally the consuming public. The flow of goods and services are in the direction of the arrows indicated in Figure 4.

The wholesalers get their supplies from the local manufacturers, the importers of manufactured, and agricultural commodities, and the private farmers and government agricultural farms. Some wholesalers are termed "processing wholesalers". These people are needed to handle the necessary pre sale processing, and bagging of such agricultural products as rice, beans, maize, and millet. They buy directly from the farmers, government agricultural farms and importers of agricultural products. These processing wholesalers sell to the distributing wholesalers who, in addition to what they get directly from the manufacturers, importers, private farmers, and government agricultural farms, needing no elaborate processing, sell to retailers, consumer cooperative societies, and the supermarkets.

The consuming public is free to purchase from any of the three groups of retailers, supermarkets, and cooperative societies, who will be required to be as competitive as possible for the overall benefit of the consumer.

An important feature of the system is that everyone acting as a marketer will be required to get registered with the government. This is not to be a punitive measure, nor a barrier to entry. Rather, it is to facilitate the categorizing of the marketers into the various marketing institutions, and line of products. This categorizing will be useful in the allotment of lock-up stores which will be differently equipped according to the needs of different categories of marketers. An individual can only be registered as either a wholesaler or retailer. If wholesaler s/he could only be registered as either "processing wholesaler" or "distributing wholesaler" Wholesaler or retailer, a marketer will only be registered for specific line of products. Thus, a marketer of agricultural products, for example, will still need to decide into what line(s) of agricultural product s/he likes to be registered. Automatically, s/he is excluded from being registered for manufactured products.

Figure 4: Flow of Goods and Services

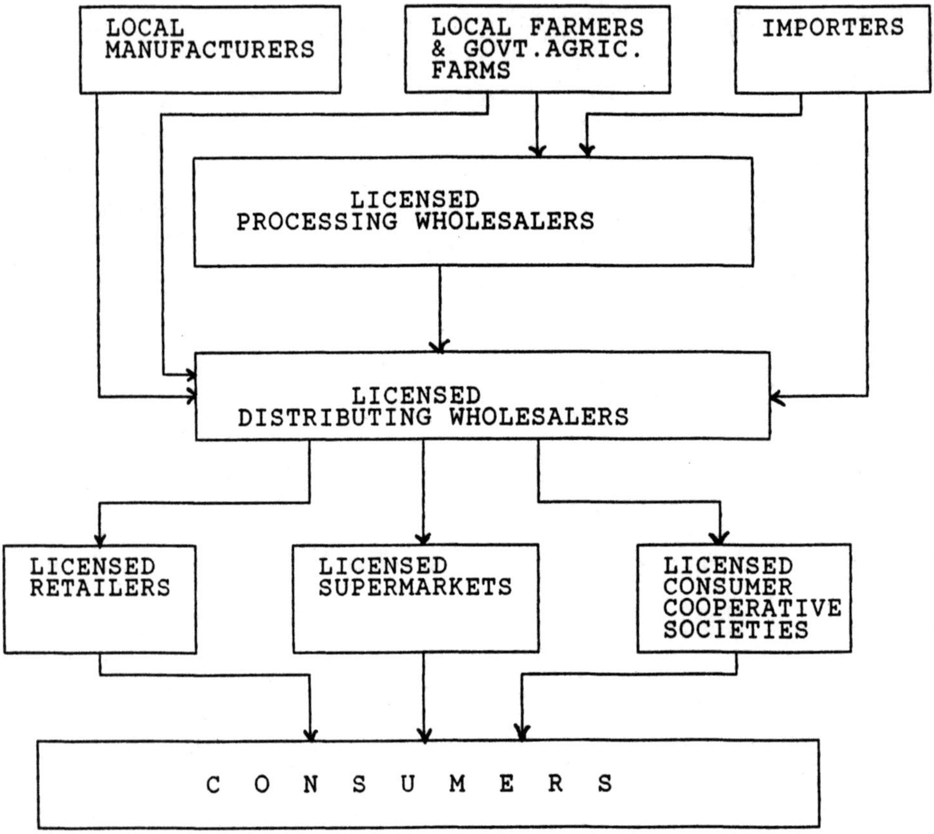

The consumer cooperative societies, as well as, the supermarkets will be registered as economic entities, while the shop operators will only be mere employers. These societies and supermarkets are allowed to trade in multiple lines of products, but can only be registered to sell on retail.

Any marketer can change his line of products and/or his or her status as wholesaler or retailer, if s/he deems it fit, only that the former registration will be annulled to create a new registration of the current status.

The only restriction to getting registered will be age. Only adults, 18 years of age and above, will be allowed to register and dually issued a registration card.

Under aged children are often ill-equipped for full-time commercial activities. They usually lack the needed knowledge, experience, and fund. In addition, allowing them to enter into the commercial world at a tender age may not encourage them to pursue their education, or apprenticeship to any reasonable level.

In the modernized traditional system, street hawking will be disallowed, thereby saving the economy of all the inefficiencies associated with this practice. All registered marketers will be required to operate in approved public market places or private stores in commercial zones of each locality. To be able to materialize this measure, the government will be required to build lock-up stores, in strategic places, all over the federation according to the local needs. These stores are to be rented out at subsidized prices to registered marketers only. The market site will designed in such a way that dealers in the same line of products will be put together. Signboards will be available to indicate the various sections of the market.

A general map of the market layout will be mounted at all the entrances to the market place for easy consultations by shoppers and suppliers alike. This will considerably reduce time spent on shopping.

Depending upon the line of products sold in a section, the stores in the section will be equipped with refrigerated warehouses, the size of which will depend upon whether the warehouses are meant for wholesalers or retailers. In all circumstances, wholesalers will be grouped together differently from retailers, as their needs in terms of space, water, and electricity supplies will differ.

Every marketer at wholesale or retail level will be required to display his/her prices for each item for sale clearly. These prices should be arrived at after a calculated allowance might have been made for a desired profit margin. For food items such as yams, vegetables, meat, rice and beans, they should be sold at a given price per kilo. Modern weighing machines should be sold or rent out to dealers in such products at subsidized prices. This method will eliminate the haggling system along with all its inefficiencies, The system of price display is already employed in the Nigerians supermarkets.

Thus, the technique is not as totally foreign to the country as to be impossible to practice. On their own part, the supermarkets will be encouraged to open branches in small towns and villages like the commercial banks are now doing. This will enable the rural dwellers to benefit from their more modern services.

Under the proposed marketing system, marketers will be encouraged to form marketers' associations according to level of operation (wholesale or retail), and line of products dealt in. Consumer cooperative societies and associations will be encouraged. These associations will encourage mutual helps, and exchange of opinions among people of common interest, and serve as a united front to ask for aids and/or redress from the government.

The modernized traditional marketing system will have to be managed by the government through appropriate organs. Suggested organs, and their functions are detailed in the next subsection.

5.2 Management Structure of the Modernised Traditional Marketing System

For effective management of the modernized traditional marketing system, three important governmental organs will need be inaugurated. These include a National Marketing Authority (NMA), a Nigerian Marketing Task Force (NMTF), and a National Bureau of Marketing Research (NBMR).

These organs and their functions are schematized in Figure 5.

The National Marketing Authority (NMA hereafter), will be charged with the construction of markets., with adequately equipped lock-up stores, all over the federation. It will ensure that constructions of the markets are based on local needs and not on political motives, A balance between nearness to the sources of supplies, and residential areas will have to be carefully worked out.

The maintenance of the constructed markets, of their stores and equipment, as well as, their public toilets will be the responsibility of the NMA. The NMA will be authorized to demand extensions of the canalization of pipe-borne water, and of tar roads, to its market sites, from the ministries of Works and Transports. It will equally be authorized to demand an extension of electricity supplies to these sites from the National Electric Power Authority (NEPA).

The NMA will be charged with the formulation of policies, rules and regulations relating to marketing practices in the country. In this task, it will consult with the Ministry of Justice for guidance so that its formulated regulations and policies will be in accord with the national constitution. It will be the responsibility of the NMA to register, and issue an official registration card, free of charge, to every marketer in the country, according to level of operation and line of product/service dealt in. Consumer cooperative societies and associations,

Figure 5: Management Organs and their Functions

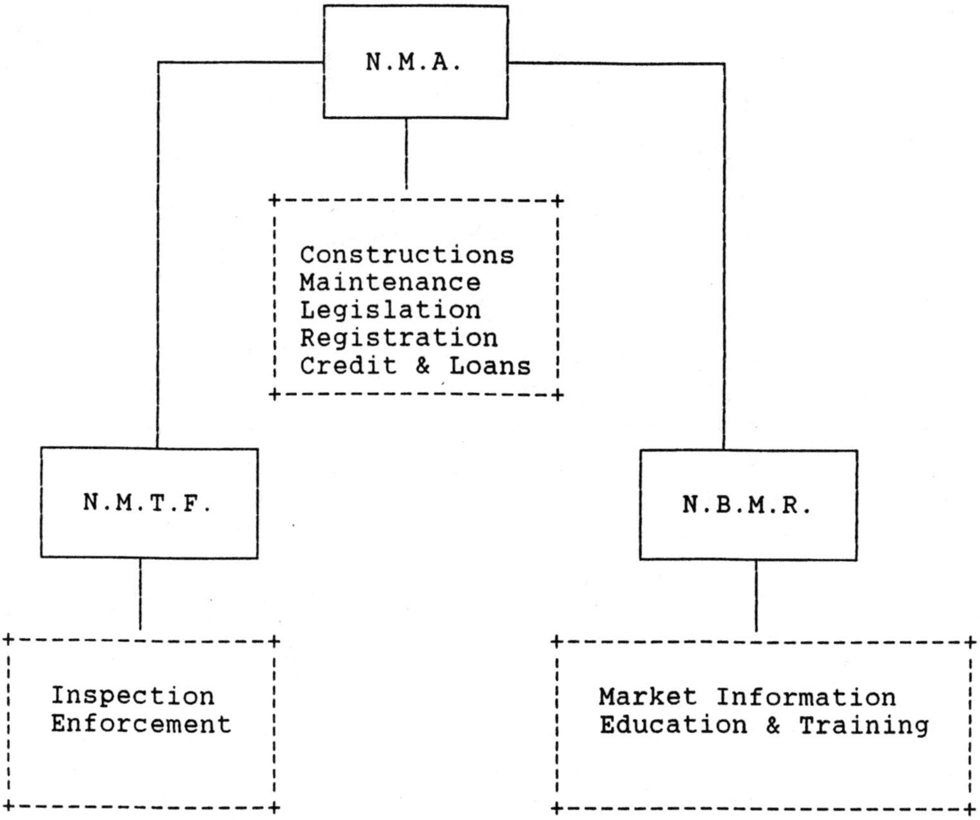

Key:

N.M.A	=	National Marketing Authority
N.M.T.F.	=	Nigerian Marketing Task Force
N.B.M.R.	=	National Bureau of Marketing Research
------------	=	Function boundary

as well as, supermarkets and marketers' associations will also be required to register with the NMA. Registration with the NMA will be a requirement to get allocated lock-up stores and any requested aid or redress demanded from the NMA.

The NMA will be authorized, and equipped to grant credits and loans to duly registered marketers, marketers' associations, and consumer cooperative societies. This is to encourage worthwhile projects, such as, purchase of modern processing plants, trucks for transportation of products, and business expansions. It is suggested that credits and loans are interest free in the first year, and be subject to half interest rate in the second year. This strategy will both encourage business expansion, and quick repayment of granted credits and loans. A marketer will have everything to gain by paying up within two years. As individual marketers or groups of marketers expand, a stage may be reached where they want to become industrialists in the line of products they formerly dealt in. This is in harmony with the activist theory that says that marketing stimulates economic development, and such marketers should be encouraged. The NMA will strongly recommend such aspiring industrialists for the loans and services of appropriate government organs, such as the Nigerian Industrial Development Bank (NIDB), and the Nigerian Bank for Commerce and Industry (NBIC).

It is recommended that the NMA be an autonomous governmental body with its own separate budget instead of being placed under such ministries as the ministry of agriculture and natural resources. It should have branches all over the federation, and be headed by a executive chairman under whom will serve directors of various tasks entrusted to the NMA.

The Nigerian Marketing Task Force (NMTF hereafter), will have the inspection and law enforcement duties under the new marketing system. It will be charged with the enforcement of the policies, rules, and regulations as may be released by the NMA. It will be empowered to arrest any defaulting marketer or association for court actions. It may recommend suspension of the registration of such defaulters to the NMA, and may take actions to seal up their stores for a determined period of time. The NMTF will ensure, at all times, that every marketer deals only in such line of product and at such level of operation for which s/he was registered.

The NMTF will be charged with the inspection of market constructions and maintenance. It will see to it that contractors perform according to the letters of the contracts entered into with the NMA. The NMA will ensure that copies of such contracts are deposited with the NMTF. The NMTF can recommend punitive actions against defaulting contractors, such as, blacklisting them, or down-cutting the payments they expected to be paid them by the NMA.

The NMTF will be the forum to deposit complaints by marketers, associations, and consumers, one against the other, and any of them against the NMA itself. The NMTF will be empowered to deal with these complaints, referring more difficult cases to the court of law. It is recommended that the NMTF be an independent, but not autonomous body. In other words, it enjoys independence of operations, but get budgetary allocations from the NMA. It should have branches all over the federation, with site offices at every market location to make it easily accessible to the people, and to facilitate its own task. The NMTF should be headed by a Director General under whom will serve directors of its various operations.

The National Bureau of Marketing Research (NBMR hereafter) will be charged with the gathering, and dissemination of marketing information all over the federation. It will also assume the responsibility of organizing and executing education, and training programs for marketers all over the country.

For effective operation of the new marketing system, adult literacy classes would need be organized for the illiterate ones among the marketers. It is suggested that these people be taught how to read and write only in the languages they speak well already and not compulsorily in English. Training programs, in various languages of the federation, will be needed to teach marketers, such things as, the use of modern weighing machines, and calculation of profit margins to arrive at the fixed selling prices to be displayed on their products. Publicity, advertising, and sales promotion technics will be taught the marketers. Depending on their line of products, the marketers will also be taught modern preservation technics to prolong the shelf-life of their products.

The training program will also be used to explain NMA's policies, rules, and regulations to the marketers, as well as, how to abide them. Procedures of obtaining redress, credits, and loans from the NMA will also feature in the training sessions. It is recommended that training programs, and literacy classes be free. The only requirement for participation should be registration with the NMA.

The NBMR will conduct regular market, and marketing research, collecting data on available and forecasted demand, and supply for different lines of product. Current and forecasted price information will be gathered and disseminated by the

NBMR. The producers and marketers will be interested in potential market for new outputs and the expected returns. Consumers will be interested in alternative shopping possibilities with regards to qualities and prices of given products. Transporters will need information on volume of passengers per market route, as well as, potential new routes under construction, or consideration by the NMA. Depending upon results of researches on areas of potential supplies, and sizes "of residential areas, the NEMR will advise the NMA on the need for, and adequate locations of new markets. The NBMR will also conduct opinion researches to gather marketers', and the public's reactions to the policies of the NMA, The impact of these policies on consumers and businesses, once instituted, will also need be assessed by the NBMR. It will advise the NMA on necessary lines of actions based on the results of such researches.

In addition,. the NMA may demand the NBMR to conduct such other market researches that it (NMA) may deem needed from time to time.

In order to make the results of its researches, and information gatherings readily available to the public, it is suggested that the NBMR publishes a journal which may be entitled the "Nigerian Marketing News". This journal may be monthly, or quarterly but should be available in the various Nigerian languages, in addition to English. The journal should be readily available at every newspapers stand at a most subsidized price. The NBMR will normally make use of copies of the "Nigerian Marketing News" in its training sessions, to teach marketers how to consult, and make use of the marketing data and information it contains.

In addition to publishing the "Nigerian Marketing News", the NBMR should also make regular marketing broadcasts on the radio, and television, in the various Nigerian languages in addition to English. These broadcasts will necessarily be shorter, but more frequent (say weekly) than the "Nigerian Marketing News".

Like the NMTF, it is recommended that the NBMR be an independent but not autonomous body. It will enjoy independence of operations, but get budgetary allocations from the NMA. It should have branches all over the federation. It will be headed by a Director General, under whom will serve directors of its various operations.

6 Conclusion

Researches have shown that marketing can be, and has been a useful tool to economic development. There is a great potential for market development in Nigeria, which development can in turn induce economic growth.

The suggestions that we have given in this chapter to modernize the country's traditional marketing system have been given after taking into consideration the technological, and socio-cultural backgrounds of the country. They are, thus, suggestions that are "tailor-made" to the needs and capacities of the country.

We strongly encourage the powers that be to give a serious consideration to the establishment of the suggested MODERNIZED TRADITIONAL MARKETING SYSTEM, and inaugurate the suggested organs (the NMA, NMTF, and NBMR) for its effective management. The result of this wise action is *induced,* and *sustained* economic growth in the 3rd republic - - and beyond.

Notes

1) Alexander, Alec P. (1960), "Industrial Entrepreneurship in Turkey: Origins and Growth" *Economic Development and Cultural Change* July, pp 349-65.
2) Alexander, Alec P (1968), "*Merchants and the Recruitment of Industrialists" in Markets and in Developing Economies*, Reed Moyer, and S.C. Hollander (eds)(Homewood, IL: R.D. Irwin, pp.190-208).
3) American Marketing Association (1983), "AMA Board Approves New Marketing Definition" *Marketing News*, 19 (March) p.l.
4) Anderson, D.A. (1970), Marketing and Development: The Thailand Experience, (*East Lansing Bureau of Business and Economic Research*, Michigan State University)
5) Arndt, J. (1972), "Temporal lags in Comparative Retailing", *Journal of Marketing*, 43 (Oct.), 40-45.
6) Cundiff, Edward W. (1982), "A Macro-marketing Approach to Economic Development" *Journal of Macro-marketing*, Spring, pp.14-19
7) Cundiff, E.W and Marye T. Hilger (1979), "Marketing and the Production-Consumption Thesis in Economic Development", in *Macro-marketing: Evolution of Thought*, George Fisk, Robert W. Nason, and Phillip D. White

(eds). (Boulder: Graduate School of Business Administration, University of Colorado).

8) Currie, L. (1968) "*Marketing Organization for Underdeveloped Countries*" in, Moyer, and Hollander (ed.) op cit
9) Drucker, Peter (1958), "Marketing and Economic Development", *Journal of Marketing*, 22 (Jan) pp. 252-259.
10) Duhaime, C.P., R. McTavish, and C.A. Ross (1985), "Social Marketing: An Approach to Third World Development", *Journal of Macro-Marketing*, 5 (spring), pp. 3-13.
11) Food and Agricultural Organization (1976), *Government Marketing Policies in Latin America*, (Rome: F.A.O.)
12) Glade, W; and Udell, J.G (1968), "*The Marketing Behaviors of Peruvian Firms: Obstacles and Contributions to Economic Development*" in Moyer and Hollander (ed), opcit, pp. 153-169
13) Hansz, James, E. and Goodnow, James O.(1973), "*Environmental Determinants of Overseas Market Entry Strategies*", in Alexandrides, C. G (1973)(ed) International Business systems Perspectives (Atlanta, G.A.: School of business Administration, Georgia State Univ., pp 195-215).
14) Hilger, Marye T. (1978), "Theories of the Relationship Between Marketing and Economic Development: Public policy Implications", in Whites, Philip D and Slater, Charles C (ed)(1978) *Macromarketing: Distributive Processes from a Societal Perspectives*; An Elaboration of Issues, (Boulder: Graduate School of Business Administration, Univ. of Colorado).
15) Hosley, Suzanne, and Chou Hou Wee (1988), "Marketing and Economic Development: Focusing on the Less Developed Countries" *Journal of Macro-marketing*, Vol.8, N0.1, spring, pp.43-53.
16) Kinsey, Joanna (1982), "The Role of Marketing in Economic Development", *European Journal of Marketing*, vol. 16, No.8, pp. 64 - 77.
17) Layton, R. (1981), "*Modeling Trade Flows in a Developing Region*", Paper Presented at the 61th Annual Macro-marketing conference, Emory Univ., Aug. 13-16.
18) Miracle, M.P. (1968), "Market Structure in Commodity Trading and Capital Accumulation in West Africa", in *Moyer and Hollander*, (ed), op cit. pp. 209-227.
19) Moyer, Reed (1968), "International Market Analysis", *Journal of Marketing Research*, 5(Nov.), pp. 353-360.

20) Nnolim, D.A. (1979), "Marketing as a Tool of Economic Development", in Julius O. Onah (ed)(1979) *Marketing in Nigeria,* (NY: Cassel Ltd. pp.7-21.)

21) Nwokoye, Nonyelu G. (1981), *Modern Marketing for Nigeria,* (London/NY: Macmillan Publishers).

22) Odia, S.G. (1979), "*Marketing: The Neglected Managerial Function of a Booming Economy*", in Julius O. Onah (ed), op cit p.3-6.

23) Papenek, Gustave F. (1962) "The Development of Enterpreneurship" *American Economic Review* (May), pp.46-58.

24) Preston, L.E.(1968), "*The Commercial Sector and Economic Development*" in Moyer, and Hollander (ed.), op cit, pp.9-23.

25) Rostow, Walt W. (1965), "The Concept of a National Market and Its Economic Implications" in Bennet P.D. (ed)(1965), *Marketing and Economic Development,* Chicago: A.M.A., pp.11-20).

26) Slater, C.C. (1969), "Marketing Processes in Developing Latin American Society", *Journal of Marketing*, 32(July), pp.50-55.

Chapter Seven

THE MILITARY AND NATIONAL INTEGRATION IN NIGERIA

Bamidele A. Ojo

This chapter examines the role of the Nigerian military in building a national consensus and at integrating the diverse socio - political and economic forces in the Nigerian Politics. The study is carried out, first by attempting to construct a conceptual framework within which our analysis will be done and second, by critically examining the successive military regimes, in an attempt to create a pattern, within contest of our earlier framework.

Our analysis will attempt to de-emphasize, the conception that, the Nigerian military is nationalistic, anti-corruption and puritanical. The Nigerian military in its recent history has demonstrated that it is as more, divided as and if not more decadent than other social - political or economic groupings within the society. It have served as agents of instability through its recurrent intervention, which has resulted in a lack of institutionalization of viable political process and institutions. The study finds the military regimes to be an infringement of democracy and neither do they represent the masses. It is in fact established that the Army often lack the diplomacy, rationale and people-oriented intellectual acumen needed for political leadership and governance.

And the military when it intervenes under the pretext to provide solutions, destroys more than it builds. The military therefore, rather than being an integrative force, has become an agent of political instability. In fact, doomed to failure by a crippling defense budget, prohibitive cost of abortive economic innovations and inexperience of its rulers, a nation ruled by the military finds it impossible to go through radical changes and achieve sound social and economic welfare of all.

The study however concludes on the note that for progress in all spheres of Nigerian socioeconomic and political development, the immense sum of maintaining the upkeep of the Nigerian Army and the incessant intervention of the military in politics must be challenged, questioned and controlled.

INTRODUCTION

"If the present states (of Africa) are not to disintegrate, it is essential that deliberate steps be taken to foster a feeling of nationhood. Otherwise, our present multitude of small countries could break up into even smaller units. Perhaps based on tribalism."[1]

Most African states have made only modest progress toward consolidating the multitude of diverse and often conflicting ethnic groups within their territories, into stable national communities. In fact, efforts have been made by some leaders but despite these commitments to instill a sense of national identity, the allegiance of a large portion of African people to particular ethnic groups still surpasses their loyalty to the national community. The attainment of a greater degree of inter-ethnic accommodation and national integration therefore constitutes one of the most critical political problems facing most African states today.[2]

It is an aberration for the Army to intervene in politics and there has been varying reasons given for this phenomenon. The Military itself has given reasons why they have had to intervene and this include among others, the need to stem the breakdown of law and order and the corruption that permeates the society. But the military itself, has more often than not been an obstacle to political and social change, rather than an agent of modernity and national cohesion.[3]

A strand of the student of the military in politics[4] argue that there are certain characteristics inherent in the nature of modern military organizations, which disposes the military to intervene in politics. And that through their training, the military acquires certain unique qualities such as puritanical, ethnic, professionalism, dedication, nationalist ethos and an in-group cohesion, which will make it act in unity, and decisively in its respective political and military functions. This school further emphasizes the uniqueness of these qualities acquired in training coupled with a high sense of national identity, managerial ability as well as, the fact that the military is recruited from the middle and lower middle classes which goes to explain its unity, strength and decisiveness.[5]

But to Toyin Falola and Julius Ihonvbere, [6] the nature of military intervention on the African continent as well as the performance of the military in office have disapproved every idea this school has advanced. According to them, the school appears to have been heavily influenced by the structural Organization and contemporary role of the military in advanced capitalist societies. They further argue that the Janowitz school does not appear to capture the fundamental basis of military intervention in peripheral capitalist social formations which belies their reliance on attitudinal, institutional or cultural approaches to the comprehension of the motives behind coups.[7]

The question is, if the military is truly united, why then do we have counter-coups and numberless abortive coups? Why do we have coups resulting from divisions within the military either in the form of hierarchy, i.e. Junior officers vs. the Senior officers, or in the form of the Navy vs. the Army or the Air force vs. the Army?. The claim to administrative superiority has been questioned also because the military, for example in Nigeria has always depended on the civil service for formulation and implementation of its policies. On the question of nationalism, experience bears out the fact that the military is as prone to corruption as any other segment of the society. All these claims and the fact that the military possess managerial skill cannot be supported by empirical fact.[8]

During the Colonial period, the Army worked on the side of the colonial state. It practically worked against the independence of the colonies. It is obvious from colonial policies of the pre-independence period, that the Army never attracted the best talent neither were they recruited from the middle and lower middle class as claimed by this school. The Huntington School[9] emphasizes the nature of the society in general, in its own attempt to explain military intervention in politics. According to Samuel Decalo, this particular school stresses societal and structural weaknesses - institutional fragility, systemic flaws and low levels of political culture, which act as a sort of magnet to pull the armed forces into the power and legitimacy vacuum.[10]

It is necessary to note that the nature of political institutions is conditioned by the mode of production, argued Toyin Falola and Julius Ihonvbere, and they went further, that the use to which societal institutions are put cannot be divorced from the accumulative base of the dominant social classes, and the class struggle in society. They believe that the gap between the rich and the poor, the corruption in high places, the rural-urban migration, the rate of unemployment and underemployment, the erosion of institutional legitimacy, the low level of social integration, the minimal or absence of political participation and the absence of a strong and dynamic bourgeoisie cannot be brushed aside, as the Huntington School attempts to do.[11]

Despite the various other reasons given for military intervention in politics, there is an agreement on the fact that, it is not only undemocratic but that there is a need to end this phenomenon as a means toward promoting political and economic development in these societies. And as the Nigerian society searches for means towards promoting socio-political and economic development. The question of national integration becomes very important as we examine the role of the military in the development of the Nigerian nation.

INTEGRATION: CONCEPT AND STRATEGIES

Defined by J. Coleman and Carl Rosberg, integration is the "progressive reduction of cultural and regional tensions and discontinuities.... the process of creating a homogenous political community"[12].There is no universally acceptable definition of integration but there is a generally agreed parameter of the concept which according to Leo Binder, involves the creation of a cultural ideological consensus of a very high degree of comprehensiveness.[13] As the definition varies, so does the strategies for achieving integration. E.H. Haas and P.C. Schmitter, for example, have suggested that the primary requisite for integration is that, the political actors involved in the process should behave rationally, with rational behavior being defined as that which seeks to maximize the payoff, to individual participants.[14]

But Coleman and Rosberg in *Political and National Integration in Tropical Africa* put forward a much more limited strategy.[15]

Their strategy involves first, the bridging of what they call an "elite-mass" gap and secondly the forging of what they term "territorial integration". The elite-mass gap which is the gap between the modernizing political elite and the traditional mass, is, according to Coleman and Rosberg, "generic to the Afro-Asian world.. (and) it is the core of the issues of national integrating these states."[16] And once the gap is bridged, the result will be "the development of an integrated political process and a participant political culture".[17] In view of the foregoing, it is pertinent to critically examine the role of the successive military administration, since 1966 and the question of national integration.

THE POST INDEPENDENCE POLITICAL CLIMATE

Nigeria's attainment of independence on October 1st 1960, was received with worldwide acclaim and the expectation that the new nation would eventually emerge as a model of unity and strength in a developing continent, that was plagued and bristling with internal strife and instability. But contrary to these expectations, Nigeria inherited some of the problems that would later throw her into imbalance and near extinction.

Nigeria, was plagued with "a deep seated imbalance in its political situation aided and abetted by a group of self seeking politicians who placed **ethnic** (emphasizes those of the author) loyalties before national interest and solidarity."[18]

The precipitant of the military adventurism in Nigeria, is a product of the colonial policies of the pre-independence era. This legacy coupled with the dependent nature of the Nigerian economy has been identified as the framework from within which the post-independence socio-political and economic situation in Nigeria emanates. The economic performance of Nigeria following independence justified to a certain extent, the hope that she would hopefully be the giant of Africa. The national income grew at an average of over 5% then, which was quite an achievement for any developing nation, although the fruits of this economic expansion was unduly concentrated in the hands of a few top politicians.[19] Moreover, the satisfactory economic progress and the general relative economic prosperity was not matched by an appreciable level of political stability.

The pre-independence election of 1959 left a permanent scar, on the body politic, which the joys of independence could not heal. The division of the political ruling class was mainly along regional lines - the Northern Peoples Congress (NPC) in the North, the National Convention of Nigeria Citizens (NCNC) in the East and the Action Group (AG) in the West. There is also the Action Group Crisis of 1962 which marked the turning point, in Nigeria's political life. The subsequent state of emergency in the West followed by the uneasy rule by the NCNC/UPP United Peoples Party Coalition Government and then the Nigerian National Democratic Party (NNDP) ushered in political tension and violence.

Other political crises included the 1962 Western regional stalemate, including the census controversies of 1962 and 1963 and the 1964 federal election, which resulted in the constitutional impasse. The degree of political tension was manifested during in the General strike of June 1964 which began as a protest by the workers and almost converted into a 'political crisis' by "those bent on seizing power at all cost".[20]

There was a continuing crisis of confidence among the accepted political leadership and subsequent political realignment of political grouping that emerged from the series of crises, included many personalities who has been discredited by a large section of the Nigerian public. The Public, according to the Federal Ministry of Information publication *Nigeria 1966* was moreover equally restless with the widespread corruption and abuse of office by highly placed persons.

It was in this climate of general disillusionment with the political ruling class that certain officers in the Nigerian Army sought to use the Army created for defense of the fatherland and protection of the citizens, to attain purely political ends.

But the tragedy in using the Army to resolve purely political questions (through military coups) usually bring in its trails tragic episodes in which violence and cold-blooded murder are the order of the day. However, the atmosphere of large scale corruption and the blatant rigging of elections, *precipitated* the January 15th 1966 military coup. Despite misgivings which many people had about the nature of the coup, it was generally well received.

First Military Coup and Ironsi's Administration

The first coup was carried out by some young majors, in the Nigerian Army, led by Major C.K. Nzeogwu. Though the coup was effected by killing some highly placed politicians, it failed to assume the power it had wrestled from them. The only source from which the objectives of the coup could be determined was in the broadcast over Radio Kaduna on Saturday January 15th by Major C.K. Nzeogwu who despite the failures of his colleagues in the South, had successfully taken over power, in the North. He declared in the name of the Supreme Council of the Revolution of the Nigerian Armed Forces that,

> "...the aim of the revolutionary Council is to establish a strong united and prosperous nation free from corruption and internal strife. Our method of achieving this is strictly military..."[21]

A major achievement of the coup was that it ended the acrimonies of the corrupt politicians. However, the reforming zeal of the young officers was snuffed out by the senior army command. And into the power vacuum created crept General Aguyi Ironsi, who in his immediate actions and policy statements gave life to the presumed the fear of Igbo domination. Notwithstanding the evidence of partisanship in the planning and execution of the January 15th coup and the doubt which existed, the coup was received by the Nigerian public as a welcome end to a corrupt regime. But the subsequent actions of Ironsi's administration further undermine the national integration. Among these actions are:

-The appointment of civilian advisers and chairmen of important departments which were predominantly of Igbo descent, thereby reinforcing the diversities within the society.

-Promotion within the ranks of the armed forces were made with a definite bias - in favor of the Igbo officers, thus out of 21 promotions in April 1966, 18 were Igbo officers.

-The promulgation of Unification Decree 34, of May 1966 which abolished the federal system had far reaching political and constitutional repercussions.

These actions more than reinforced the fact that the Ironsi's regime is not an integrative force. The decree for instance, altered the basis of the Nigerian political system and was done without adequate consultations. The riots and violence that followed, further led to the deterioration of the already worsened situation in the country. The ethnic wound was further widened. And what was considered as a counter-coup produced the events of July 29th 1966, which led to the fall of Ironsi's government. The north led coup culminated in the change of administration and the assumption into office by Lt. Col. Gowon, as the head of the federal military government and supreme commander of the Nigerian armed forces.

THE GOWON ADMINISTRATION

This government made by far the greatest effort at integration.

At the beginning, Gowon was confronted with the task of reconciling the different ethnic groups and integrating the country into a united and stable nation. Realizing the immense political and constitutional problem confronting the country, he (Gowon) immediately set the machinery in motion for finding a lasting solution to these problems. He undertook:

- The release of Chief Obafemi Awolowo, the leading Yoruba leader. He was the leader of opposition in the federal parliament until his imprisonment in 1963. He also released other political prisoners and detainees.
- An immediate return to the federal system of government, in view of his recognition that, over-centralization processes inherent in Decree No 34 virtually brought the country to the verge of a civil war.
- the establishment on September 12th 1966 of an Ad-hoc Conference on constitutional proposals comprising representatives of all the regions of the federation, to determine the issue of state creation and maintenance of political stability.

The creation of more states has always been a bone of contention in Nigerian politics even before and since independence. The ethnic composition of the three regions which existed at the time of independence and the resultant fear of domination led to the creation in 1964 of the Mid-West Region. And upon the recommendation of the Conference, the federal military government had to create new states by decree on May 27th 1967. In his broadcast to the Nation on a new program for a United Nigeria, on November 30th 1966, he gave the principles for the creation of new states as:

- No one state would be in a position to dominate the central Government.
- Each state would form one compact geographical area.
- Administrative convenience; the fact of the history, and the wishes of the people concerned, must be taken into account.
- Each state should be in a position to discharge effectively the functions allocated to regional government.
- It is also essential that the new states should be created simultaneously.[22]

Twelve states was created by Gowon's administration. This decree was well received by the vast majority of the people. But the damage has already been done by the past administration and the counter-coup of July 29th. The Igbos was under attack in the North and driven back to their region. Lt. Col. Ojukwu, the military governor of the eastern state was not in support of the state creation, which would have reduced his ability to command the East, in its eventual secession.

The Eastern Region on May 30th 1967 seceded when Ojukwu illegally declared the region a sovereign state - The Republic of Biafra. Although several efforts were made at reconciliation but it all failed. The civil war lasted until 1970. Gowon emerged from the civil war much stronger than he has ever been and he was able to cultivate both domestic and foreign support by a judicious handling of rehabilitation, reconstruction and reconciliation programs. This was also aided by the oil wealth which Nigeria experienced with the petroleum boom. In an effort toward national integration, he announced in October 1970 a disengagement program, wherein he promised to address itself to some critical problems facing the nation before returning power to a civilian administration in 1976.

Some of these programs included the eradication of corruption, the conduct of a national population census, the organization of election and the inauguration of a popularly elected government at the states and national level. This program was not only ambitious but it provided the nation a sense of purpose and was widely received. It also provided the basis for evaluating the regime's performance but only two of these programs received attention during the life span of the regime namely the national population census and the issue of corruption.

As the bases for economic development and revenue allocation representatively, the census in Nigeria has always been controversial. The military carried out its own census exercise in November 1973 and the distribution by state was seen to be contrary to demographic theories and further widened the margin between the southern and northern states, thereby creating further mistrust and increased antagonistic views from the South. The Daily Times (of Nigeria)confirmed this in one of its editions when it said:

> "A census exercise whose outcome does not enjoy public confidence is a wasted effort... these unchecked figures have caused a greater deal of depression, anger and fear among several sections of the Nigerian community.."[23]

Corruption was an elusive problem to document and the performance of the administration on this was adequately summarized by the *Sunday Sketch* (of Nigeria) of July 28th 1974. When "Eselby" on the Tarka/Daboh issue indicated that:

> "...There is no doubt that Mr Tarka's continued presence in the federal executive council is not a good advertisement for a Government which claims to be serious about checking corruption in the nation's body politic..."[24]

By this time, it was apparent that the return to civilian rule in 1976 as promised by the regime was unrealistic.

Murtala-Obasanjo Administration

Ironically, Gowon was removed on the ninth anniversary of his accession to power, his Government fell to another group of soldiers, led by Brigadier Murtala Mohammed, who felt Gowon's regime was purposeless and has merely discredited military rule. But it must be mentioned that Gowon's administration was a major step towards national integration, with its reconciliatory drive, the revival of the Nigeria Unity despite the war, the creation of more states, the restoration of federalism and establishment of National Youth Service Scheme (NYSS) - an effort to instill in Nigerian youth the sense of patriotism.

However, Brigadier Mohammed's maiden speech, after the coup of July 29th 1975 summarized the shortcomings and the areas in which Gowon has failed, as an integrative force. According to him,

> "...After the civil war, the affairs of state hitherto a collective responsibility, became characterized by lack of consultation, indecision, indisciplined and even neglect. Indeed, the public at large became disillusioned... the leadership either by design or default had become too insensitive to the true feelings and yearnings of the people the nation was thus being plunged inexonerably by chaos.."[25]

The new regime took some dramatic and fundamental decisions which included retirement of officials (public officers) either for old age, incompetence and abuse of office, etc. The administration canceled the 1973 controversial census and created seven new states. The decision to move the federal capital out of Lagos, to Abuja was taken. In fact, these swift decisions were to be the hallmark of the administration. In its bid toward national integration, the administration introduced a common land use law, and local government reform throughout the country. And it set up panels for constitution drafting and the constituent assembly to consider the drafted constitution was composed.

The Murtala-Obasanjo regime was committed to handing over to an elected civilian government in 1979. In fact, it believed that:

- the long military rule had created a myriad of problems for the army such as proliferation and division among top officers, unnecessary political ambition, quest for political offers to make wealth and diversion from the primary goal of defending the country against external aggression.
- Gowon's bankrupt administration and indecision over disengagement had contributed immensely to discrediting the army.
- the transition could curb unnecessary ambition for counter-coup.[26]

Despite the assassination of the head of state, General Murtala Mohammed on February 13th 1976, by an abortive coup led by Lt. Con. Dimka, the administration under Gen. Obasanjo went ahead with programs by lifting the ban on politics and finally handing over power on October 1st 1979.

Buhari-Idiagbon Administration

Approximately four years and 3 months after the Obasanjo administration handed over power to a civilian government, under the presidency of Alhaji Shehu Shagari, the news of another coup reached the public, in the early hours of December 31st 1983. Between 1979 and 1983 there was corruption in high places, unemployment and nepotism. Moreover, the west(western Nigeria), because of the belief that its presidential favorite lost the election which was presumed "rigged", did not support the central administration and has always looked forward to a change in the leadership of the country.

In the statement of Major General (then Brigadier) Sanni Abacha, who accused the Shagari administration of imposing "grave economic predicament and uncertainty" on Nigeria. According to him:

> "...I am referring to the harsh intolerable conditions under which we are now living. Our economy has been hopelessly mismanaged. We have become a debtor and beggar-nation. There is inadequacy of food at reasonable prices for our people, who are now fed up with endless announcements of importation of food stuffs... yet our leaders revel in squandermania, corruption and indiscipline continue to proliferate public appointment in complete disregard of our stark economic realities."[27]

In an effort to justify their intervention the head of state, Major-General Buhari, while addressing the world press conference in Lagos on January 5th 1984 emphasized the gross mismanagement on the part of Shagari's administration and according to him:

> "..The otherwise buoyant economy of the first two fiscal years, 1979 and 1980 was allowed to run down through mismanagement."[28]

The General also accused the various governments of the defunct second republic of having "failed to provide even the minimum of good government and unable to deal decisively with fraudulent acts, arson at public buildings, corruption, indiscipline, smuggling, armed robbery etc."[29]

In the opinions of Toyin Falola and Julius Ihonvbere, the Buhari administration and its prescription for Nigeria's problem were divisionary, escapist and reflective of the petty bourgeois right-wing character of the coup. However, this administration, through its decisive pretext, and rigidity cultivated the antagonism of some sectors of the society i.e. workers, students, journalists, doctors, academics. In fact, the rigidity of this administration was best exemplified in the nature of the decree it produced - despite popular advice the regime went ahead and promulgated decrees which rather than solving problems created new ones, i.e. Decree 20, under which several drug pushers were killed despite national and international opposition.

One might consider crediting this administration with instilling, within the short period, a sense of nationalism, discipline, and dedication to duty. This was carried out, through its war against indiscipline programs.

BABANGIDA'S ADMINISTRATION

The change of guard was announced by Brigadier Joshua Dongoyaro on August 27th 1985. The removal of the Buhari-Idiagbon leadership is no doubt a result of conflict within the supreme military council. This rift divided the hard-line clique of Major -General Buhari and Idiagbon from the rest. "Despite its numerical inferiority, the Buhari-Idiagbon alliance muscled through" and this alienated the government from the people.[30]

According to the new head of state, Major-General Babangida who was Buhari's chief of defense staff, the Buhari administration;

> ".. was too rigid and uncompromising in his attitude to issues of national significance..." and he said of General Idiagbon arrogated to himself absolute knowledge of problems and solutions and acted in accordance with what was convenient to him, using the machinery of government as his tool."[31]

Major-General Ibrahim Babangida, has been involved in three coups and a member of the Buhari's supreme military council. In his attempt to legitimize his regime, he released political detainees, repealed dreaded decree No 4, released a British businessman - thereby making an important gesture to Nigeria's major trading partner - Britain. The new government faced a lot of problems, among which is the problem of Nigeria's membership of the Organisation of Islamic Conference (OIC), International Monetary Fund loan, and many others. Its national debate on OIC undermine the fragile sense of national unity because of the socio-cultural divide in the country.

The Government in its attempt to portray a government ready to listen to peoples' contribution, open many of these issues, some rather sensitive, for public debate. The most appalling attempt is that of the OIC which generated some outcry from many quarters. This administration also set in motion earlier on a disengagement program. Its failure not to honor the result of June 12 1993, which paved the way for national unity because of M.K.O. Abiola's potential victory by receiving votes from all corners of the country. Its annulment of the election and the public outcry that followed greatly undermined the integration of the Nigerian society.

Coup Plot against Babangida

Late December 1985, witnessed the minister of Defense, Major-General Domkat Bali, announcing the government's successfully preventing a coup. And on March 5th 1986 ten of the officers found guilty by a military tribunal for their roles in the abortive coup were executed. This list includes, the Soldier-Poet, minister of capital territory (Abuja) and member of the Armed forces Ruling council (AFRC), Major-General Maman Vatsa and many other strategists and first-class air force men.[32](Considered a coup by the Air Force). In his speech, Major-General Bali emphasized the problems of coups by saying categorically that "The point must be admitted, that seven coups in 20 years in this country are just too many for the stability and orderly progress of the society."[33] He emphasized the unlikelihood of investors investing in Nigeria in case of another coup and also believed that, because of the coup, it is going to take a long time before mutual trust and confidence can be restored in the armed forces.

The Abacha Administration

The Babangida administration went on to register two political parties and followed it up with elections to local, state and national offices but as it dawned on his administration that a southern Yoruba but Moslem businessman M.K.O Abiola was on his way to winning the election, the results were annulled. Abiola provided the example that democracy can survive in Nigeria in spite of ethnic differences. The cancellation of the election in fact did more harm than any other act by the military because it seriously undermine any form of inter-ethnic trust that may exist in the country. The outcry forced Babangida to resign and he left behind a transition government under Ernest Shonekan but he in turn was removed in a palace coup led by General Abacha, his defense minister.

General Abacha on assuming power dedicated himself to handing over power in 1996 then 1998. When Abiola tried to claim his mandate a year after the annulment, he put him in prison.

When former heads of States and leaders protested his style of governance, he put them all in prison. From General Obasanjo to General Yar Adua (who died recently in prison(January 1998) and recently his right hand man General Diya is in prison for planning a coup. Despite his commitment to handing over power in 1998, the outside world and the Nigerian society is clearly monitoring the transition process because of the possibility of Abacha running as a candidate and because of his human rights records which has greatly undermine the integration process. He will always be remembered for the hanging of Ken Saro wiwa and the prosecution of the Ogonis.

Conclusion

It has become so normal for the military to be in power in Nigeria thereby preventing political evolution within the Nigerian society. They have intervened and without any ideological or purposeful plan halted, the necessary process of institutionalization and evolvement of a political culture in the country. For Ironsi, he saw the integrative process in largely formalistic and symbolic terms.[34] It reasoned that once the forming of the "amalgamated community" is legislated into existence, the behavior that gives an ontological reality to the form should follow.[35] It was in this spirit that the Ironsi regime abolished the federal structure and instituted in its place a unitary state. There was recruitment from the bureaucratic-managerial elites in an attempt at operationalizing the goal of the unitary state. In the process, the paradigm of managerial government was substituted for the politics of consensus and accommodation. But the outcome was the alienation of those members of the elite who felt their interests were not sufficiently catered for. They therefore communicated their deprivation to the masses, thereby leading to discontent and withdrawal of support for the regime.[36]

With the experience of the Ironsi regime before it, it was only to be expected that the successor regime of General Gowon would seek to remove the policies initiated by Ironsi. Gowon's administration was the first successful attempt into national integration but the structural incoherence of the military then made it impossible to effect strategies for final integration. In a federal society like

Nigeria, with weak loyalties to the central institutions, the problem of leadership becomes crucial. Gen. Mohamed's administration succeeded in transforming the image of the federal Government. This was due to its decisiveness, its impartiality in its decisions and a transparent insensitivity to sectional political pressure. This was also manifested in the Buhari administration. The regime had exploited, like Murtala's administration, the unified command structure of the military to control the activities of the state governors but unlike Murtala's administration, Bubari's failed to set examples for them to follow.

It is generally obvious that popular support for the central government may be a function of the leadership in fashioning an impartial image for itself. It was a general contention that the Buhari administration created the impression that they were angels, and for example it sentenced the former Governor of Plateau State, Mr Solomon Lar, to a 21 years jail term (through one of its tribunals) for spending 30 million on security for four years, while he, Buhari, was believed to have spent 600 million in one year![37]

This is the military and the dwindling economy of Nigeria.

President Babangida was quoted in the Guardian(of Nigeria) of Sunday March 30th 1986 that he had a vision of a military, that will henceforth keep away from government. He said that

> "The idea is to try now to make every officer come back, settle down, and let us look at our role as past defender of the country and compare it with the role we have been playing now and the question is shall we be able to continue to play these roles, keep ourselves to the role we have been assigned by the constitution or did we see ourselves doing both which put necessarily leaving one thing or the aspect of the Organisation to suffer."[38]

According to him:

> "I feel if we have a real good system, we should be able to in this country have government without necessarily bringing the military in to do it.." And that "ours will probably be the last intervention of the military in the political system in the country."[39]

Babangida's vision was personal and like all military officers, was ready to quit but there are others who would like to be called President and there are those who dream of more of it

Despite these earlier position, Babangida went on to contribute immensely to this problem by annulling the June 13 Presidential election thereby denying the people's mandate and endangering the process of national integration. Being forced to resign and with his friend Abacha in power, his prediction seem to have an ironic reality to it because fifteen years after, the third republic is not yet a reality.

The Military incursion in Nigerian Politics has rendered the political process in the country non-existent. Without coups, probably, there would have been a process of evolving viable and stable politics. We shall not know. And not until the military is questioned and challenged about their hegemony to rudely intervene is politics. Not until then, shall we have a stable political and integrative process. In fact the most important desire of every society is to be able to provide the basic human needs required for the advancement of the society.

The ILO World Employment Conference of 1976 defined basic human needs to include;

"...certain minimum requirement of a family for private consumption, adequate food, shelter and clothing... certain household equipment and furniture... services provided by and for the community at large, such as drinking water, sanitation, public transport and health and educational facilities.. the participation of the people in making the decisions which affect them... employment... both as a means and as an end. Employment yields an output. It provides an income to the employed. And it gives a person the recognition of being engaged in something worth his while..."[40]

This should be the desire of every successive government in Nigeria. But both civilian and military alike are engrossed in corruption, nepotism and mismanagement. The military for instance lacks the nationalism, puritanical tendencies and orientation to manage the Nigerian economy. The military has made the most monumental of all decisions in post-independent Nigeria. It has govern the longest term (28 years of 38 years). The military in Nigeria is more of an agent of instability rather than an integrative force. And this phenomenon cannot be attributed to the post independent military and constitutional structures and developments alone. It is also a product of:

- The capacity of the Military to interpret that a plural society is positively correlated with its own internal cohesion.
- And the less bureaucratic and ideological the military, the greater is its chance of success in integrating a plural society.[41]

Also the classical division of the military as a cohesive group derives partly from the conception of the military institution as a prototype of Weber's ideal bureaucratic organization and partly from the assumed impact of the processes of socialization into military roles upon its individual members. However, the recruitment policies into the army by the British before the independence (based on regional quota of 30 - 25 - 25) opened the army from the to regional conflicts and ethnic rivalries. The absence of recruitment and promotion by merit, at this epoch, also damaged the organizational structure of the Nigerian Army.

The Nigerian experience and the inability of its military to carry out effective integration is a product of the division inherent within the rank and file of the Nigerian Armed forces.

NOTES

1) Julius Nyerere: *Freedom and Socialism* (London: OUP 1968) p209.
2) David Smock: *The Search for National Integration in Africa* (New York Free Press 1976) p.3
3) Aldo H. Solari and S.M.Lipset (eds): "Elites in Latin America" in I.L. Horowitz *Military Elites* (New York: OUP 1967) p.151, 178-190
4) Moris Janowitz: Military Institution and Coercion in the Developing Nations [expanded edition of] *The Military in the Political development of New Nations* (Chicago: Univ. of Chicago Press 1977).
5) John J. Johnson ed):*The Role of the Military in Underdeveloped Societies*(Princeton, NJ: Princeton University Press, 1962).
6) Toyin Falola and Julius Ihonvbere: *The Rise and Fall of Nigeria's Second Republic* 1979-1984(London: Zed Books, 1985)
7) Ibid

8) Ibid
9) S.P.Huntington: *The Soldier and the State* (Cambridge: Harvard University Press, 1967). Also S.P.Huntington: *Political Order In Changing Societies* (New Haven:Yale University Press, 1968)
10) Samuel Decalo: *Coups and Army Rule in Africa: Motivations and Constraints* (New Haven: Yale Univ. Press) p.7
11) Toyin Falola and Julius Ihonvbere: *op cit*
12) J.Coleman and Carl G.Rosberg (ed*): Political Parties and National Integration in Tropical Africa*_(Los Angeles:UCLA_Press, 1964) p9.
13) Leo Binder: National Integration and Political Development: *America Political Science Review* Vol 18, No 3, Sept 1964, p650
14) E.Haas and P.Schmitter: Economic and Differential pattern of Integration: *International Organization* Vol. 18, No 17, Dec. 1964, p.711-719.
15) Coleman and Rosberg: *op cit* p 686.
16) Coleman and Rosberg*: op cit.*
17) David Smock: *op cit* p3l.
18) *Challenge of Unity*:(Lagos: Federal Ministry of Information, 1967)p1.
19) Nigeria - 1966: (Lagos: Federal Ministry of Information, 1966)p4.
20) Ibid.
21) Text of Broadcast: Taken from Ruth First "Coup of Young Majors", *The Barrel of a Gun* (London, Longman, 1970), p285.
22) Nigeria - 1966 *op cit* p50.
23) *Daily Times*, Lagos, (Nigeria) June 8 1974.
24) "Eselby", *Sunday Sketch*, Lagos, (Nigeria) July 28 1974, p2.
25) Brig M.Mohammed: Text of Maiden Broadcast to the Nation as reproduced in the *Daily Times*, Lagos, (Nigeria) July 31, 1975, p3.
26) Toyin Falola and Julius Ihonvbere *op cit.*
27) Brig Sanni Abacha, Text of the Coup Broadcast to the Nation, Dec 31 1983, quoted from Toyin Falola and Julius Ihonvbere, *op cit* p230.
28) Major General M.Buhari, Address to a World Press Conference, Lagos, Jan 5, 1984, Quoted from T. Falola and J. Ihonvbere, p230.
29) Toyin Falola and Juilus Ihonvbere, *Ibid.*
30) *Concord Weekly* Lagos, (Nigeria) No 57, 12 Sept 1985.
31) A Renewal of Promise: *Concord Weekly*(Nigeria) Issue No 57, *ibid.*
32) *Vanguard*, Lagos, (Nigeria) Thursday March 6th 1986, Nigeria.
33) *Vanguard*, (Nigeria) Ibid p5.

34) B.J.Dudley: Military Government and National Integration, in Smock and Benlsienchill (eds): Search for National *Integration in Africa*, (New York: Free press 1976
35) B.J.Dudley: Ibid
36) B.J.Dudley: Ibid p42.
37) Personal View - Mbadwe Eimelumba; *Vanguard*, Lagos(Nigeria), Tuesday 8, April 1986, p9.
38) *Guardian*; Lagos, (Nigeria) Sunday March 30 1986.
39) Ibid.
40) *Economic and Social Consequences of the Arms Race of Military Expenditure*: UN Publication E72/IX.16, Quoted from J.O. Ihonvbere, Unpublished paper presented at a one-day seminar on peace and disarmament, Feb 1986, Univ of Ife Ile-Ife "Meeting Basic Needs as a Grass Root Approach to the Quest for World Peace".
41) Olugbemi S.O.:"Conflict and Consensus in Nigeria's Military Regime", Paper presented at the Symposium on the Political process within Military Regimes. Centre d'etudes des Relations Internationale of the Foundation National des Sciences politique, Paris, May 17 - 19 (1979).

Chapter Eight

Structural Adjustment, Corruption and Politics in Nigeria

Peter Agbese and Julius Ihonvbere

In the present military era, corruption has become all pervading, unabashed, uncontrolled, unavoidable and persistent.[1]

We thought the civilians were corrupt. compared to the current military regime, Umaru Dikko and his friends were saints. This regime has no shame. It will go down in history as the most corrupt regime Nigeria ever had. The only lesson they are teaching Nigerians is that it is good, in fact, great to be corrupt. [2]

In this chapter, our main objective is to document the place and role of corruption in both the adjustment and political transition program. It is essential to do this for three main purposes. First, we hope to explode the myth and mistaken belief that the Babangida regime is less corrupt than any other regime or administration in the country's history. Second, we hope to show that the adjustment program actually increased the tempo of corruption as the Nigerian bourgeoisie virtually went wild with the devaluation of the Naira. The adjustment program was all that was required to convince the bourgeoisie that there was an economic crisis and the intensified struggle that followed was to corner whatever resources was left. Finally, third, we hope to show the implications of such rabid corruption and patterns of primitive accumulation for state power, political relations, consensual politics, and economic recovery in Nigeria.

It is always difficult to define what exactly we mean by corruption. For a working definition, we accept Ekekwe's definition of corruption as "the process of obtaining material enrichment or opportunities for the same, for oneself and/or for others, through the use of public office (or influence) in ways other than those publicly acknowledged through the rules and procedures of that office".[3] This definition includes all forms of nepotism, bribery, abuse of office, inflation of contracts, kickbacks, peddling of influence, name dropping, manipulation of laid down rules, bending the rules, threats issued in order to achieve ends which otherwise would not have been achieved and so on. Of course, we recognize that in societies like Nigeria, where as a result of the limited commodification of production factors and forces and the prevalence of strong cultural influences, the separation between the modern and the traditional, and between the private and the public, the identification and determination of what constitutes corruption can, at times, be very difficult and in most cases very tenuous. Yet, the difficulty noted above should not deter us from trying to study and understand the role of corruption in the numerous crises confronting Nigeria. We hasten to add, that we do not by any means, unlike Larry Diamond and Richard Joseph, regard corruption as a primary explanatory variable in the discussion of contradictions, crisis, conflicts and underdevelopment in Nigeria. For, us, corruption is a manifestation of the weaknesses of the local bourgeois class, the weak role and place of the state, the structure of production and accumulation and the generally weak nature of economy and society. We also do not regard corruption as an exclusively elite affair. Though, we do believe that the Nigerian bourgeoisie is mostly responsible for encouraging corruption and in protecting corrupt elements within the system. As well, because the state has been inconsistent in prosecuting corrupt persons and enforcing anti-corruption laws, it has inadvertently encouraged the spread of corruption to all nooks and corners of the society. More importantly, given the state's inability to meet the basic needs of the people in an increasingly difficult and hostile economy and society, people have come to rely on illegal, unorthodox, extra-legal and corrupt mechanisms to survive. To be sure, the spread of corruption has been encouraged by mass poverty, unemployment, the abuse of power by the elite, the rehabilitation of corrupt individuals and criminals by the state, the neglect of the rural areas and vulnerable groups and the general impression encouraged by the state that without connections with somebody in power, life would remain virtually impossible. Yet, we make bold to say that the Nigerian elite has found these developments only convenient to cover its tracks of indiscipline, waste, mismanagement and corruption. It has also found it expedient to rely on cultural explanations to rationalize corrupt acts.

Another point that needs to be made is that corruption within the ranks of the Nigerian elite is neither a post-colonial phenomenon nor was it caused by the structural adjustment program. In the pre-colonial era, while as a precipitate of the communalist relations of power, production and consumption and the fact that most production was for use rather than exchange value, corruption was very limited, it experienced an expansion under colonialism. This was largely because of the deprivations and marginalization suffered by the indigenous bourgeois elements in the hands of the colonial state and metropolitan bourgeoisie. The majority of the emerging bourgeoisie had to resort to corrupt practices to survive the competition, win access to the market and to compete with foreign capital. But the period before political independence saw the increasing reliance on corruption as a mode of accumulation. As soon as the local power elite captured political power in October 1960, corruption and corrupt practices became the primary mechanism to accumulation and personal enrichment.

Eme Ekekwe has argued that, even if illegal, and quite unorthodox, corruption can be seen as a "means of accumulation". This is largely because, in any capitalist system, corruption, no matter how rationalized or sophisticated, is one means to accumulation. How rampant, widespread and sophisticated it is, is dependent on the character of the state and bourgeois classes. More importantly, bow the loot is used, in other words, whether it is invested or squandered or stored in foreign lands, is also dependent on the character of the dominant classes and the environment in which the class operates. As Ekekwe notes:

> While there is no denying that corruption is highly visible in post-colonial societies, I find rather inadequate the attempts made to explain it by linking it with tradition and custom. Furthermore, I do not think that corruption is a moral problem and I do not think that it is necessarily a hindrance to bourgeois development,
>
> ...I consider corruption as a valid, if illegal, means of accumulation. This is not to say that I therefore approve of it. Not at all. Corruption creates for those who engage in it, an economic opportunity. It is not necessarily antithetical to development in the conventional sense of that word... Corruption necessarily exists in and is encouraged by, every capitalist economy, since, in such an economic system the drive and competition for private profit and capital accumulation are the motor.[4]

The point which Ekekwe does not consider is that socialist societies have all been plagued with widespread corruption. In addition, while it is true that accumulation through corruption provides those who engage in it with "economic opportunity", the reality is that in the Nigerian case, this "opportunity" has not benefited the country in any way. As we shall show shortly, accumulation through corruption has been one major factor in the country's deepening crisis and mounting foreign debt profile. Of course, contract inflation, tax evasion, manipulation of sales figures, forgeries, direct stealing, over-invoicing, influence peddling and other forms of corruption are rampant in all societies.

But while the looting of the funds of a local government can cause severe damages to production, education, services and facilities and so on, the savings and loans scandal in the United States involving, among others, Neil Bush, the son of the American President, George Bush, which is costing the American economy some $500 billion has not had a similar effect. This is largely because the American economy has the capacity to absorb major frauds and in any case, the stolen wealth is recycled and reinvested within the United States.

Thus, corruption in Nigeria has been generated, sustained and reproduced by six major factors: First, the unproductive and dependent character of the Nigerian elite which has come to rely on the state and the stealing of public funds as the easiest avenue to accumulation, As Ekekwe has rightly noted, "for the Nigerian governing class, development was synonymous with personal enrichment, and that the use of state power for this process was theoretically and practically accepted by them... state power.... once achieved was used for personal gain".[5] The second factor, is the weakness of the state. The Nigerian state has never been taken seriously when it claims to abhor corruption or when it declares its intention to control corruption and punish offenders. This is largely because all the structures and institutions of the Nigerian state are filled with corrupt personnel. There is hardly a Nigerian leader or politician who has not been publicly accused, found guilty, or censored for involvement in corrupt practices. Thirdly, the Nigerian economy is dominated by profit and hegemony-seeking transnational corporations. It will be foolhardy to think that these transnational interests have the interest of the Nigerian society at the top of their priorities. Their main goals are profit, control and market hegemony. If in the course of their operations they confront a very indiscipline, decadent and corrupt ruling class that is willing, with little or no encouragement to subvert laid down rules and regulations on behalf of transnational interests for a little reward, they take advantage of it. Again, Ekekwe has rightly argued that the domination of the Nigerian economy, "places a severe limit on the normal process of private accumulation for indigenous capitalists - a process exacerbated by the low level of the development of the productive forces".[6] The only way to accumulate available to the marginalized local bourgeois elements is to collude with foreign capital or to take advantage of the weakness of the state to divert public funds into private bank accounts. The fourth factor has to do with the character of society - the completely perverse culture of waste, decadence, ostentation, addiction to foreign tastes and irresponsibility. The interests among the elite, the so-called educated Nigerians, urban dwellers and youths to glorify wealth irrespective how it In acquired has contributed immensely to corruption in Nigeria. This culture of practically worshiping wealth, the get-rich quick mentality, the belief in "plenty money with little work", the urge among youths to ride the best cars and live in luxury has promoted the booming drug trade in Nigeria and legitimized corruption. It is shocking that in contemporary Nigeria, tales of corruption 1 hardly shocks anyone. In fact, the response one often gets is "go and get your own share". As Sully Abu rightly notes, "Corruption is today a forgotten word, even if the press tries to dredge up the subject. Few eyebrows are raised when the word is mentioned and few still when it is used specifically in relation to a government official or other public servant. The practice has become the norm, the oil business, smothering relations, inviting a smile and expected as a courtesy greeting".[7] Of course, the state has encouraged this culture of condoning corruption by turning a blind eye to illegal acquisition of wealth, conspicuous and ostentatious living, decadent and irresponsible display of wealth by persons with no visible means of income and by pretending to be waging a war against the drug and foreign exchange trafficking business. As Sully Abu notes:

> Official sanction of this state of affairs (sic corruption) would appear to have been provided by the absence of the word from official discourse or the practice from the sins to be punished. Where we have railed against 'undue radicalism', enemies of the transition program, or of SAP, sexual harassment (in the universities of course) and where we have promoted patriotism and a healthy work ethic, corruption has been conspicuously missing from the field of battle. Instead it has been well nestled in the spectator stands, The word 'corruption' has progressively been sanitized to the point of being denuded of all opprobrium".[8]

The way in which military officers, customs officials, politicians, senior police officers and "emergency contractors" display their wealth and flout it in the hungry faces of disadvantaged groups has further fueled the growing greed in society and the preference for enrichment by cutting corners. Fifth, is the condition of poverty and uncertainty. When a people have very little to fall back on and very little hope for the future, they become very vulnerable to corrupt practices. They give bribes to the police to stay out of trouble, they prefer to bribe the courts and police rather than spend their life savings on hiring a lawyer, they bribe school principals to get their children into schools even if the children had passed the entrance examinations, they bribe meter readers from the electricity corporation to cut their meter bills rather than pay to the state, they bribe airline ticket sellers to purchase flight tickets in order to travel from one city to the other, there is hardly a day a Nigerian does not offer a bribe for one thing or the other, ideological or religious dispositions notwithstanding. Sixth, and finally, the ease with which the proceeds from corrupt practices is transferred to private bank accounts abroad, facilitate corruption in Nigeria. Greater integration of the Nigerian economy into the global capitalist system is conducive to corrupt practices in Nigeria because it provides numerous avenues for transferring corrupt proceeds abroad.

Although it is often said that corruption has become a way of life in Nigeria, since the advent of the Babangida regime and the introduction of the structural adjustment program, corruption in Nigeria has taken a new dimension. It is no longer a way of life, it: is life itself. It: is our view that this is the case for three main reasons. First, the regime itself is corrupt. One of its policies has been the rehabilitation of corrupt elements who had been probed and found guilty in the past. People like Samuel Ogbemudia and Ukpabi Asika, who were probed and found guilty by the Murtala regime and consequently "dismissed with ignominy" from their jobs were fully rehabilitated by the regime. All the military governors under the Gowon regime who were found guilty and "dismissed with ignominy" from the armed forces have had their dismissal annulled by the Babangida regime. Their military ranks which they had lost on account of massive corrupt practices have been restored to them. Given such open and unabashed flirtations with discredited and disgraced elements, the regime, to a considerable degree legitimized corruption. Secondly, the adjustment program, as in preceding chapters have shown has been a nightmare for vulnerable groups, pensioners, the unemployed and other disadvantaged persons in the country. With no alternative ways of survival, they have all turned to serving as pimps, fronts, agents and partners to thieves, blackmailers, drug peddlers, contractors, forgers, distributors and other elements who operate on the other side of the law. Of course, the middle class has been hard hit by the adjustment program. Those in positions of responsibility with access to public funds, seeing the impacts of adjustment on the poor and the middle class, simply looted away at the treasury ostensibly to take care of the future. Today, every one in Nigeria is looking for some public money to steal or some government department to defraud. Many regret that they failed to steal or corner their respective shares of the "national cake" or "oil boom bonanza" before the burst and adjustment.

Thirdly, the regime, in spite of adjustment and the decline in foreign exchange earnings has openly and deliberately fueled corrupt practices through the way it spends money. It bribes journalists, creates all sorts of openings for people to have access to public funds and enrich themselves, and reshuffles its governors and ministers so rapidly that it has become clear that part of the reason is to give' every military officer a go at the state treasury. Furthermore, the regime rehabilitates persons dismissed from one arm of the government for corrupt practices in other arms, has no policy on accountability and takes accusations against serving officers as a joke: "misapplication" of funds has officially replaced "corruption", "embezzlement" and "misappropriation. " It is a regime that has thrived in sponsoring all sorts of jamborees, festivals and one where wife of the President as well as the wives of military governors, through the Better Life for Rural Dwellers' program and other projects, spend public funds as if they were direct employees of the state. These wives, donate public monies on behalf of government even when they have no votes or constitutional powers to do so. It is a regime where less than a quarter of the hundreds of appointments it has made since 1986, have been based on merit but on direct or indirect connections or the desire to silence criticism and opposition. What is interesting however, is that it is under this regime that for the first time in the nation's history, state commissioners were resigning in protest against the corrupt practices of governors under whom they served. In addition, it is under this regime, again for the very first time in the country's history, that a nation wide riot culminating in the mass destruction of lives and property was sparked off by allegations of corruption against the President and his wife.

Let us look at specifics of corruption in contemporary Nigeria.

CORRUPTION AND ADJUSTMENT

In Nigeria's first republic, 1960-66, corruption was widespread. The politicians were loud about their illegal modes of wealth accumulation and the openly encouraged their supporters to engage in such corrupt acts. The location of public projects, resource allocation, public appointments and so on were determined on the basis of what the politicians and ministers could get through backhand deals. When Major Nzeogwu and the majors struck in January 1966, corruption indiscipline and mismanagement were, together, perhaps, the major excuse for their intervention. The Gowon regime was even more corrupt than the civilians of the first republic. Gowon lacked the power to control the bourgeoisie. He was himself deeply involved in protecting corrupt public officials and in spite of allegations and scandals, he was unable to discipline his officials in any way. In fact, the stamping out of corruption, which was one of the "Nine-Point Program" announced towards the hand over of power to civilians in 1976, was merely a paper declaration. When he was overthrown in 1975, a whole sordid world of corruption and indiscipline was unearthed by the Murtala administration. In the full-scale probes initiated to look into the assets and conduct of public officers, Nigerians were shocked at the revelations: nine of the military governors and the Administrator of East Central State, Ukpabi Asika, were found to have abused their offices, looted their treasuries and mismanaged public funds in an unprecedented manner. In his historic broadcast to the nation announcing the report of the probe, General Murtala Mohammed declared; this panel has examined the assets of the former Military Governors, the former administrator of East-Central State and some former federal Commissioners. The details of the decisions on each of the former public officers so investigated will be announced immediately. Suffice it to say that all the ex-Military Governors and the former Administrator of East Central State with the exception of two were found to have grossly abused their office and guilty of several irregular practices. Clearly this investigation has revealed that they had betrayed the trust and confidence reposed in them by the nation. Those of them who wore uniforms betrayed the ethics of their professions and they are a disgrace to those professions. They should be ashamed of themselves. They are therefore all dismissed with gnominy and with immediate effect.[9]

With the assassination of General Mohammed in February 1976, the open commitment to financial probity and accountability was virtually terminated. To virtually all those dismissed by the Murtala regime, have been rehabilitated without being cleared by any court of law. Under General Olusegun Obasanjo, took over from Murtala Mohammed, the most celebrated case of corruption was N2.8 billion oil money scandal. In spite of a Tribunal of Inquiry set up by the Military Government and chaired by Justice Ayo Irekefe, the scandal was never resolved. Though the Tribunal claimed that the missing money was not paid into a private account as it had been alleged, it unearthed numerous cases of corruption in the oil industry and in institutions with business dealing with the industry.

The civilian administration that succeeded the Obasanjo regime has already gone into the records as perhaps, until now, the most corrupt in the country's recent history. The administration made more money from oil sales and yet, accumulated more foreign debts. The legendary Umaru Dikko Affair, the rampant purchase of private jets, the Johnson Mathey Bank scandal, the importation of custom made wines and all sorts of nefarious connections with Swiss banks were just some of the features of this era. Chief Arthur Nzeribe, one of Nigeria's millionaires has claimed in a recent publication that in 1983, he submitted a list of Nigerians who had illegally stashed away $16 billion in foreign banks to the President, Alhaji Shehu Shagari. The list showed that "most of the account operators are civil servants, military officers, Government functionaries of al cadres, retired and serving. How and where did they make the Money?"[10] Nzeribe's list was comfortably neglected and nothing was done to investigate the assets of those whose names appeared on the list. A prominent politician made a profit of N140 million from deals involving the Federal Government. By the time the administration was over thrown in December 1983, corruption had become a way of life.[11]

The two generals, Buhari and Idiagbon, who succeeded the Shagari regime, throw scores of politicians into jail, set up tribunals to probe and try them for mismanagement and corrupt practices and left no one in doubt about its total commitment to probity and prudent financial management. The regime did not live long to implement its policies. It was overthrown, due to "irreconcilable differences" in a palace coup master-minded by General Ibrahim Babangida. The Babangida regime began by releasing all the detained corrupt politicians. It followed this up by the open rehabilitation of discredited politicians and military officers and by appointing such persons to positions of responsibility. Thus now, the trend which actually started in the colonial era, and was strengthened in the first decade of political independence has become perfected and virtually consolidated as part of the mechanisms of political, social and economic operations. As Arthur Nzeribe has noted "what has worsened the issues of corruption.... is the present government's indifference". He went further to contend that; "Indeed one will be hard put to find a public statement in which Babangida has devoted any attention to the issue of corruption in Nigeria... the military is the most hypocritical, deeply corrupt institution in the country".[12]

Let us take a look at a few examples since it will take volumes to document such blatant acts of corruption.

Accusations against the President, his wife and his Chief of General Staff (CGS), Augustus Aikhomu, culminated in a nation wide riot in 1989. The President was alleged to have stashed away over $500 million in foreign banks; his wife, Mariam was alleged to be operating, among other business interests, several expensive boutiques in France and a businessman, Alhaji Mohammed Bashir, alleged that the Chief of General Staff, defrauded him out of $500, 000 being kickback on an oil deal. He went to court and swore to an affidavit providing the be account numbers of the CGS's account into which the kickback was paid, In spite of widespread riots and destruction of lives and properties, the accusations of corruption have not been successfully explained away. In the case of the CGS, t security forces arrested Alhaji Bashir and detained him without trial. Later, secret deal was struck, and he was released without ever being brought to court at least as a lesson to others for making false allegations against the second in-command. A few months after the Alhaji's release, the CGS was 'cleared' by Nigeria Police which has an international reputation for corruption.

Then, there was the case of the military Governor of Borno State, Col. Mohammed Maina who was merely retired from the army with his loot. As Governor of Borno state, he refused to attend meetings in Lagos and practically kept a 1 his loot to himself. In Nigerian parlance he "failed to settle". Maina was alleged to have spent N9 million in 24 hours to host the Prince and Princess of Wales when they visited his state. When the wife of a senior official of the administration visited the state to attend a "Better Life for Rural Women" event, the governor spent N100, 000 on the brief visit. When the governor attended the burial ceremony of the late Brigadier Dan Archibong in Calabar, he squandered N500, 000. Any time he attended a meeting in Lagos, he carried with him a minimum amount of N300, 000 in cash. He had no patience for accounting procedures and was reported to have made withdrawals from the state account by sending "brief notes to accounting authorities at the Treasury". When the

President visited the state capital Maiduguri, the governor again squandered N2 million on the six hour visit. Any time he had cause to travel out of the state, he used chartered flights: he was too big and too important to travel in the same aircraft with other Nigerians. He presided over the award of petty contracts including those within the competence of local governments such as contracts for the construction of motor parks.[13] For all these crimes and more, the governor is not in jail today, he was not properly probed, his assets were not seized by the state and he was not dismissed from the army. In fact, the former Chief of General Staff, Vice-Admiral Augustus Aikhomu, later a civilian Vice-President in the regime claimed that "Col. Maina did not embezzle money, stressing that there was a difference between embezzlement and mismanagement".[14]

It is instructive to note that Borno state is one of the poorer states in Nigeria with a low literacy level, high infant mortality rate, high unemployment and with about three-quarters of the population living below the poverty line. The Governor can hardly point at a single achievement that can be attributed to his administration. Yet for the financial indiscipline, theft and sqandermania, all he got from the Babangida regime, was retirement with full benefits. If Governor Maina was corrupt, he was a new comer to the game of corruption in the Babangida regime. In Cross River State, navy Captain Ibim Princewill presided over a harem of graft, inefficiency, indiscipline and mismanagement. The administration reveled in nothing else other than in corrupt practices and the programmed underdevelopment and mismanagement of the already poor state. His administration was so corrupt that it forced the people of the state to organize political pressure groups dedicated to his removal from office as Governor. The Cross River State Redemption Movement, led by Grace Eyo-Ita was one such organization dedicated to the exit of Princewill from the state. They eventually succeeded but not after Princewill and his men had run down the state, emptied its treasury and increased the internal and foreign debt profile of the state.

On his retirement, as usual, with full benefits from the Navy, the new Military Governor sent to the state, Lt. Colonel Ernest Attah was so appalled by the state of the economy and the depth of antagonism and popular dislike for the office of the governor that for the first time in the history of the country, a new military governor was forced to set up two probe panels, headed by Emmanuel Effang and Dorothy Nsa Eyamba-Tdem, both High Court Judges to look into the financial improprieties of his predecessor. The Justice Dorothy Eyamba-Iden Commission of inquiry which looked into the books discovered among other things that four oil palm estates at Kwa Falls, Ndasop, lbiae and Boki, had in process of privatization been undervalued.[15]

The estates, were "sold at million, N1.3 million, N5.62 million and N2.96 million respectively. At current values they should have been sold at N12.6 million, N4.73 million, N11.38 million and N6.1 million respectively".[16] The so-called privatization process of Ibim Princewill, suffered from inadequate publicity and "the whole process was 'conducted in utter secrecy and the proceeds salted away into private accounts".[17] In addition to the above, 20 contracts valued at N90 million "for which mobilization fees had been paid without work being done", were awarded bylaw the administration. Any Nigerian can tell that under such arrangements the contractor and the Governor, Commissioners and Directors General usually share the mobilization fee or the total amount of the contract.

With no work done, the contractor cannot be charged since public officials had already compromised themselves by accepting kickbacks and other bribes. The governor awarded a N56 million road contract "in Obudu, of which mobilization fee was paid, even before architectural drawings were made"; and "re-awarded another contract for which a N2 million mobilization fee was paid".[18] Ibim Princewill awarded huge contracts to non-existent organizations like Messrs Mastex Imports/Exports Limited which was supposed to be located at No. 6 Sanusi Fafunwa Street, Victoria Island Lagos.

The state accountant-general could not account for the sum of N7.8 million meant for the state and practically all the contracts awarded by the administration did not pass through the State's Tenders Board. Other corrupt acts included the over valuation of contracts, sinecure appointments and the general laxity with which budgetary allocations were disbursed. A few scapegoats have been sacrificed for some of these crimes against the people of the state. For instance, the Commissioner for Works, Dr. James Mbu was asked to refund N1 million being excess monies paid out to contractors. He was able to refund N750, 000 to the coffers of the state and he is still a free man today. Essienox Nigeria Limited, which had collected the sum of N318, 975 to "supply blinds for doors and windows of a yet to be completed Calabar Specialist Hospital" was asked to refund the money. The same instruction was issued to Flobett Pharmaceutical company which had collected N1.2 million to "supply drugs".[19] For all his misdeeds, Princewill, was merely retired from office as Governor and from the navy. Today, he is busy putting up designer houses in Buguma, his home village, Degema and Port Harcourt, all in his home state - Rivers State.

In Rivers State, there was the case of a Commissioner resigning from the governor's cabinet in opposition to waste, misplaced priorities, corruption and nepotism. Dr. Dima Denni - Fiberesima resigned from Group Captain Ernest Adeleye's administration because, among other allegations, the Governor "single handedly, without reference to the state Ministry of Health, or the state executive council (engaged in) buying medical boats for N10,876 million". In addition, the Governor often kept large amounts of money in state house accounts, which he spent without accounting to anyone. The Governor also had a habit of funding projects directly rather "than through the ministries whose duty it is to do so". In the 1990 budget, the Ministry of Health had N4.8 million approved for its capital projects but the military Governor "was to keep N36.5 million and disburse directly to the ministry". In the same budget, Governor Adeleye, allocated N7 million to the state house clinic.

The Governor never really denied these allegations. In fact, in the heat of the allegations, a newspaper The Broom published additional allegations of corruption against the governor. Copies of the paper were bought off the streets by persons who "loved the governor". Contractors, parading themselves as friends of the state, took out paid advertisements in the newspapers to defend the governor, obviously to win his attention and support for the next contract award. But while the governor refused to defend himself, security forces arrested the Commissioner, ransacked his home and office and took away his documents. In addition, the Federal Government, in typical style "cleared the Governor" of any wrong doing, promoted him to the rank of Air Commodore and redeployed him to the Nigerian Defence Academy(NDA) as Deputy Commandant. So much for Fiberesima and all those who, rather than join in the looting, busy themselves in criticizing corrupt officers.

In Ogun State, another Commissioner, Dr. Olaseni Akintola-Bello, who had served as Commissioner for Finance under Governor Mohammed Lawal, a navy captain, resigned in anger from the cabinet accusing the governor of corruption and a range of other financial improprieties. Dr. Akintola-Bello did not stop there, he took out paid advertisements in several national dailies on May 19, 1989 outlining his allegations against the governor. Amongst the allegations against the governor were "inordinate withdrawal of fixed deposits (over N40 million) from the Odua-Owena Bank and subsequent placing in a low interest yielding account with the Kwara Trade Bank Limited; the setting up of a rival treasury at the Governor's office; the payment of mobilization fees of between 50 per cent and

70 per cent on contracts; the fine tuning of the records on the state's indebtedness to facilitate the granting of N40 million loan by the First City Merchant Bank; and the use of Ogun State's funds to service Kwara State(the governor's home state)".[20] The former commissioner dared the governor to take hi to court so he would have the opportunity to open a "can of worms". He called o the Federal Government to institute a public probe into the governor's activities concluding that "I assure you that a public enquiry will open a Pandora box the will shake the governor to his foundation. It will be a can of worms". The Federal Government did not take up the challenge and the military governor did not attempt to take the ex-commissioner to court. Rather, the CGS, who is himself a naval personnel, "traveled by train to Ibadan, made a stop over at Abeokuta, and took the opportunity to announce that investigations by General Staff Headquarters had shown that the governor was not guilty of the allegations".[21] The so-called "investigations" were conducted in secret, that is if there were ever any "investigations" conducted by any one. The clearance was also suddenly announced in a hurry by the CGS without any documents made available to the public. It was clear to all Nigerians that once again, the Babangida regime was trying to cover up its track of corruption and mismanagement.[22]

In Anambra State, the former civilian governor in the second republic, Chief C.C. Onoh and the incumbent Colonel Robert Akonobi were involved in a major war over land ownership and the use of state power to retain control of certain properties. The Military Governor was accused, among other things of "unbridled acquisition of wealth, the amassing of wealth and the building of mansions in Enugu, Onitsha, and his own village, Neni".[23] In addition to the above was the "glaring opulence and how he made overnight millionaires of his relations which is demonstrated in the building of houses worth millions of Naira by people who prior to his arrival could not boast of N200 in the bank".[24] Complaining directly about how the finances of the state was being utilized, C.C. Onoh, who has himself not lived above board, noted that the "monumental corruption in Anambra state... the wealth, financial resources and federal grants being provided for the development of Anambra state by the central government have been converted into an exclusively family affair meant for Akonobi brothers a misters to the exclusion of the indigenes of the north and south".[25] While everyone in Anambra State knew that the military governor's brother was t informal "deputy governor" of the state, the governor himself dismissed a allegations against him as "baseless and unfounded." Onoh himself admits to owning 510 undeveloped plots in

Enugu. He is also alleged to own 1187 fully developed plots in Enugu urban alone". While these members of the elite are busy insulting themselves in public, wasting public resources in their attempts to intimidate one another and playing up ethnic, communal and regional differences in order to consolidate their hold on political power, the masses of the people in Anambra state continue to suffer from the adverse effects of poverty, underdevelopment, neglect and structural adjustment.[26]

Finally, is the case of Governor Bode George, another Navy Captain and military governor of Ondo State. Recent revelations showed that he probably ranks amongst the most corrupt in the country. The African Concord(Nigeria) reported that:

> Between December 1987 and last August(1990), the premises of the governor's office complex in Akure, the Ondo State capital was like a commercial nerve center. Cars of various makes and sizes with Lagos license plates thronged the complex's parking lot. From Mondays through Fridays, between 6.00 p.m. and midnight, there was heavy traffic in and around the Governor's office. Very important visitors from Lagos arrived in gleaming Mercedes Benz V-Booth cars and other exotic brands. In the inner recesses of the complex, deals were brokered, contract papers changed hands and everybody was generally happy. The visitors and the chief host laughed to jokes, watched latest video, drank choice wines and played games sometimes till as late as 4.00 a, m. the next day. During this period, Navy Captain Olabode Ibiyinka George, presided over the affairs of the state. He was the Chief Executive, the Chief Accounting Officer and the only individual who had authority to award contracts.[27]

According to the magazine, during this period, the governor "disbursed Ondo State funds with utter disregard for laid down procedures and little respect for civil service rules and regulations".[28] All over that state the governor construct fountains at a cost of N250, 000 each. Today, these fountains have become breeding grounds for mosquitoes. Most of his contracts went to particular companies which were reputable for their inefficiency and preparedness to give huge kickbacks The governor handled all contracts for the "supply of equipment and other materials to most ministries and government parastatals". He even purchased vehicles and forced local government chairmen to pay for them in cash even when such local governments were not in need for vehicles and had made no request for vehicles. A contractor friend of the governor had to find an avenue to supply something to the government. For the supply of Delphi 416 telephone system in his office, the governor awarded a contract for N77, 000. He purchased a BMW car for himself in April 1990 and shortly before he was redeployed to Lagos "cars were given to aides the way a company gives hampers to its important customers at Christmas. Even a junior staff at Government House that saw to the welfare of the former Governor's children was not left out. She was given a car as a 'parting gift'.[29] Bode George was said to have approved the sum of N617, 762.81 for drainage, stone pitching, road pavement and concreting of the main bowl of parade ground even when he recognized that an almost similar amount had been previously approved by him for a similar purpose in the past. The state government also held back part of the proceeds due to farmers from the sale of cocoa. Eventually, a contract for N381, 550.26 was awarded for the construction of a Farmers House.

In his bid to improve on his sagging image in the state, the governor, working with his press secretary printed 27, 000 copies of his portrait at an unbelievable cost of N243, 000. Interestingly, the same poster had been printed at the cost of N150, 000 for 25, 000 copies sixteen months earlier. The cost of gold and gold plated frames was not included in this bill. Yet, the Ondo State Government has a functioning printing press with capacity to print those posters for a very small fraction of the expended amount. Like his fellow naval officer in the Cross River State, Bode George's privatization program was a mere excuse to bleed the state dry and divert public funds into private pockets. The Okitipupa Oil Mill company, Ile-Oluji Cocoa Industries Limited and Araromi Rubber Estates were sold largely to non-indigenes of Ondo state, mainly to top political figures, businessmen and retired military officers. If privatization was being pursued as a strategy for rolling back the state, Governor Bode George did not appear to have understood the meaning of privatization and deregulation as part of the adjustment package. This is because as his government was selling off some very lucrative companies, it was busy acquiring over valued and decaying enterprises. From retired Major General Olufemi Olutoye, the Ondo State government bought Tolu Enterprises, a hatchery, for N3.5 million.

A few months after the purchase, the premises of the hatchery was "deserted". A house belonging to an ex-federal commissioner was purchased for N2.5 million and part of the building was converted into a Cultural Center. The rationale for the purchase, when a better and more modern structure could have been easily erected was never explained to any one. When the governor took The Broom to court allegedly for publishing defamatory news about his wife, he hired a leading lawyer for N100, 000. The first installment to the lawyer for N50, 000 was drawn from the purse of the state. The governor never repaid the money even after settling the case out of court. As Babatunde Olugboji and Babafemi Ojudu have rightly noted:

Ondo state government's accounts during the tenure of Governor George might as well have been Captain George's personal accounts, going by the way he ordered the payment of money, sometimes to a faceless contractor who didn't appear to have done any job for government... During the week beginning 20 August(1990) -his last full week in office Captain George commissioned completed, semi completed and unfinished projects".[30]

During the Easter break in 1990, the Governor abandoned his palatial quarters in Akure and his numerous guest houses including the luxurious liaison office in Lagos and checked into the expensive Lagos Sheraton Hotel with his family. At the and of a three day stay, the Ondo State Government settled the bill for N 26, 000 Finally, the governor was also behind the fraudulent purchase of three refurbished flat barges, redesigned as transport boats, and sold to the government at a total cost of N6million. In reality, the boats were hardly worth N750, 000.[31] For all these obvious crimes and more, Bode George was simply redeployed to Lagos to enjoy his wealth and leave the people of Ondo State the poorer for it.

Alhaji Sidi Ali Sirajo, who until his dismissal as managing Director of the Federal Government owned *New Nigerian* newspapers corporation was also neck deep in corruption. In so far as he fanatically defended the government his excesses and abuse of power were condoned by the regime. He was alleged to "have inflated several contracts, and to have fallen into the habit of demanding money from governors and other top personalities on behalf of the *New Nigerian*; even receiving money on behalf of his staff, which he never accounted for".[32] Like the military governors discussed above, Sirajo's case was one of collecting monies on a regular basis though unorthodox procedures, manipulating financial procedures, collecting kickbacks and mismanaging public funds. The punishment for these and other offenses was a mere sack from his job as Managing Director. In Akwa Ibom State, a commissioner collected N150, 000 from a businessman "on behalf of himself and the state governor, Colonel Godwin Abbe... but allegedly refused to mention or deliver the envelopes to the governor".[33] He was merely dismissed from office as commissioner after he was confronted with the allegation by the governor himself. If he had behaved properly, and shared the content of the envelope with his boss, the story, without doubt, might have been different.

The Federal Ministry of Defense claimed that it had run up a debt of N9 billion. It was only recently discovered, that the Ministry which has on its own created scores of millionaires and billionaires was in reality indebted to the tune of N3 billion only. Some individuals within and outside the Ministry had manipulated the books, waiting for the government to release N9 billion so they can corner the extra N6 billion. No one was blamed for this astronomical increase in the Ministry's debt profile, it has been business as usual.[34] In Niger State, 37 school principals diverted the sum of Nl,200, 000 "from school accounts kept for feeding boarding school students". All they got in return when the crime was uncovered were "disciplinary action--ranging from outright dismissal to demotion and reposting".[35] The state government in demonstrating its "anger", merely retired those who "misappropriated over N60,000", demoted seven others in rank to become classroom teachers while the others were merely "demoted by grade".[36] They were not prosecuted and today, they belong to a group of rich Nigerians who demonstrate to the youth that it is a waste of time engaging in hard work.

In Bendel state, school books worth NIOO million imported on behalf of the government by a private company disappeared allegedly from the port and ended up "the open market".[37] So far no one is in jail. An investigation into the rd of the contract in the first place will certainly implicate top public servants. In the same state, employees of the Nigerian Postal Services stole "an estimated N2. 5 million through mail theft racquet" through "the routine diversion of mail suspected to contain valuable foreign currency".[38] Today, all mails coming into the country stand only a ten per cent chance of getting to their destinations as a result of the widespread corruption in the Nigerian Postal Services.

The devaluation of the Naira which has increased the value of foreign currencies vis-a-vis the local currency, especially in the parallel market, to unprecedented levels has contributed to this corruption in a major way. Yet, no policy for checking the fraud has been mapped out and the Minister in charge of communications has so far not expressed any serious concern over the matter. The culture of corruption has sunken so deep in the society that junior staffers are not scared of embezzling all the funds of a ministry or parastatal. At the Newbreed magazine, two staffers, Godwin Chianungo and Dele Aito who were Personal Assistants to the Chief Executive, Chris Okolie, were dismissed and then charged to court, accused of "conspiracy, fraud and theft of N1.5 million property of Newbreed Printing and Packaging Limited between November 1988 and January 1990".[39] Details of the case showed a carefully planned and professionally executed program for defrauding the media house on a perpetual basis. Chief Arthur Nzeribe revealed recently that the country's Chief of Army Staff, Major General Sanni Abacha was "putting up a palace in Kano estimated to cost 200 million naira". He blamed President Ibrahim Babangida for his lackadaisical attitude towards numerous allegations of corruption in the country and for pretending that he was unaware that "as many as three Mercedes Benz cars are parked in the garages of some military lieutenants".[40]

It is not only the military that has been involved in acts of corruption oven if they have succeeded in getting away with more such acts than civilians. The Kaduna newspaper, *Today,* reported in 1988 that a former Assistant Inspector - General of Police, who had been implicated in the confessions of arrested drug - suspects in April 1985, "left an estate estimated to be worth N11 million, N2 million of which was in cash" when he died in 1987.[41] Even if Alhaji Daura ha saved every kobo he earned while alive, he would not have been able to save N1 million. Mr Justice Agbaje-Williams accused two magistrates of corruption in 1981 'when, in an address to the Annual Conference of the Magistrates Association of Nigeria he declared: "I have been receiving reports for some time, about the behavior of two of your members... Their judgements are insane, their utterance in and out of court, irresponsible. There are even whispers about their probity in relation to matters touching upon the conduct of their judicial duties".[42]

It is amazing that the Justice had received complaints about only two of the magistrates in Nigeria. Anybody in Nigeria will easily tell you that; a) once the government is involved in any case, the chances of winning a favorable settlement is one in a hundred thousand; b) once your opponent has the resources to hire a Senior Advocate of Nigeria (SAN), the case is as good as lost; c). if you were represented by a progressive or radical lawyer like Alao Aka-Bashorun, Femi Falana, Gani Fawehinmi and Olu Onagoruwa, they had to be thrice as good in their submissions and the case had to be practically obvious else it could be lost on "technical" grounds; d) if you had a case against a traditional ruler, customs officer, military officer or wealthy businessman or their relatives, friends, concubines or girlfriends, you were in very serious trouble and the chances for obtaining a favorable ruling was extremely limited; and e) such statements as "my hands are tied", "I want to get to the Supreme Court", "I will soon retire and I want to retire in Peace" and "the government has an interest in this case" all come from the fact that cases are hardly determined on the bases of arguments, submissions and facts. Akinola Aguda has been one of the very few prominent lawyers, who has been in the forefront of the struggle for a responsible, independent and corruption free judiciary in Nigeria. Traditional rulers, who today have very little to do with tradition and more to do with primitive capital accumulation, politics and the use of tradition to rationalize corruption have not been left out of the widespread corruption in the country, especially under the Babangida regime. A traditional ruler in Bendel state was killed while participating in an armed robbery operation. The police was shocked to find his bullet riddled body but managed to hush up the scandal. The Olu of Warri, Ogiame Atuwase has been accused of "illegal collection of over N400,000.... a third of the sum paid as compensation to some Itsekiri families in respect of oil spillages" in 1989.[43]

The most recent report of the nation's Auditor-General showed the extent to which the state has been bled dry, the total absence of proper book-keeping practices in most departments and parastatals and the open use of the state to accumulate capital. The report "contained cases of unpaid loans, huge loses in stock and cash plus gross abuse of official property".[44] In its examination of the nation's books, the Auditor-General found out that the Administrative Officer to the Constituent Assembly, (an Assembly whose work was practically thrown overboard by the Babangida regime) could not account for N85,000 and payment vouchers "could not be found to support the proper use of another amount totaling N292,405." Though the Assembly claimed to have expended NI.9 million on deposits for accommodation and catering to the NOGA-NICON HILTON HOTEL in hotel bills or statement of account could not be produced. There were no documents to support the alleged purchase of video sets and advances made to members of the Assembly. No one has been relieved of his responsibilities or charged to court for this sloppy book-keeping. The Nigeria Police, the haven of corruption in Nigeria could not properly account for N52,231, expenses which it claimed it "made for settling the hotel bills of only 14 officers purported to have been accommodated in Owerri in Imo State".

In the same Owerri, the Imo state Government operates a highly subsidized Catering Guest House which is open to the public with public servants enjoying preferences. In addition to the above, the Police in Imo State "misused" N750, 877 meant for the "reactivation of grounded vehicles for use in the 1987 local government elections." When the stores of the Police were inspected in Owerri, it was discovered that no vehicle part was bought or supplied. The Federal Ministry of Works and Housing could not locate 28 payment vouchers for which payments had been made and the N126,000 allocated to the Ministry for the "clearing of Koko toxic waste dump could not be adequately accounted for". Monies collected for the registration of companies disappeared into thin air.[45] Of course the N99 million scandalous Bi-Water Price Water scheme in Niger State is still fresh in the records of large scale frauds in Nigeria. Today, "not a single drop of water has issued forth" from the project which created several millionaires. Yet Bi-Water still 'wins' contract awards to supply water to villages.

With the introduction of structural adjustment and the decision to impose no, fees, levies and tolls came the decision to construct 22 toll gates on Federal highways all over the country. This would have meant, NI million per toll gate. This was to be an ordinary toll gate, nothing automatic or exceptional. Yet, the Nigerian bourgeoisie managed, in a period of retrenchment, unemployment, inflation, hunger, disease and increasing disillusionment to increase the cost of the toll gates from the original N22 million first to N54 million and later to N74 million. In 1988, the National Salt Company of Nigeria, Ijoko-Otta imported crude salt worth N2 million. This was its major raw material. Th imported salt was "adulterated with sand, rocks and cement particles". We ca also recall with ease the Lockheed scandal in which some public official "accepted bribes of about N2.5 million in a deal involving the buying of six C13 transport aircraft worth N40.6 million for the Airforce". There is perhaps n point in going on with this sordid listing of the gory story of corruption in Nigeria.

The cases cited above are just a tip of the iceberg of corruption which characterized the Babangida regime. Virtually all those involved in the offenses listed above as well as others worse in magnitude have not suffered any hardship as a result of the discoveries of fraud in their handling of public funds. In fact, many of them have been promoted, given positions of higher responsibility and were very close to the seat of power. Several of those involved in the open rip-off of the nation are among the leading political figures in the count today and they are currently presiding over the funds of the political parties. Yet, others have become advisers to Military Governors and traditional rulers. It is instructive that such open and pervading corruption is taking place at a time when the conditions of living of the poorer class have deteriorated to unprecedented levels.

Those who criticize or oppose corrupt governors or military personnel or civilians serving in military governments run serious risks. They could got eliminated, sacked, framed for all sorts of offenses, jailed, deported out of the country, detained as security risks or harassed to a point where they learn to keep quiet. The late Professor Tam David West, a former Minister for Petroleum was jailed for 20 years, not for embezzling money, but for "enriching Stinnes Interoil Incorporated of the United States to the tune of $57,117,433 U.S. dollars". It was alleged that the Professor "allowed the American oil company withhold payment of the amount to the Nigerian National Petroleum Corporation (NNPC)".[46] While David West was in jail, most probably for his trenchant criticism of the Babangida regime, of Jibril Aminu as oil Minister and of the alleged "northernization" of the oil industry, criminals who bled their states dry are either retired or promoted. In Cross Rover State for instance, Madan Grace Eyo-Eta only narrowly escaped been beaten to death recently by hired thugs for her leading role in the crusade against corruption and in particular against the corrupt administration of Ibim Princewill.[47] Patrick Wilmot, the well-known teacher of sociology, was abducted and deported from Nigeria in March 1988 by the security forces for his trenchant criticism of the double standards in Nigaria's anti-apartheid policy and the corruption and indiscipline of the Nigerian ruling class. Students have been massacred by the police and intellectuals detained for long periods for openly criticizing corruption in high places in the country. Yet, there is widespread recognition of the endemic nature of corruption in the country's body politic as well as the negative implications of corruption for national harmony, the preservation of the ethic of productivity and hard work.

As Alhaji Ibrahim Mohammed complained about the Babangida regime, "official corruption has been alleged under the present administration, and hard work has ceased to be an ideal".[48] The *African Concord* has rightly noted that as it is "almost every stratum of the Nigerian society has been immersed in the rot"[49]

Domkat Bali, the retired Minister of Defense and Chairman Joint Chiefs of Staff has equally wondered as to how military officers "come about fantastic cars" in which they cruise around the country.[50] Festus Iyayi, the former National 'President of the Academic Staff Union of Universities(ASUU) who was dismissed from his University job for leading his union in a resolute stand against human rights abuses, corruption, abuse of power and the erosion of university autonomy under the Babangida regime has equally stated that "most Nigerians got rich the illegal way".[51]

This level of corruption and political decay continue under the Abacha regime.

CONCLUSION

It is easy to hide behind the facade of culture to rationalize corruption. Thus bogus arguments are invoked to the effect that it is part of African culture to exchange gifts and to give gifts to persons who have extended one form of assistance or the other to another. These may be true. But we all know that the sort of corruption we have been talking about goes far beyond the exchange of gifts and barely has anything to do with African culture. As Tade Aina has correctly argued, "corruption is corruption. It refers to the use of the advantages of office to illegally enrich oneself either through plunder, fraud or receipts of gratification for the performance of what should have been one's normal duties".[52] Thus when Colonel Raji Rasaki, Military Governor of Lagos State "received a gift of a hundred cows for the burial of his mother', he was being corrupt. In Nigeria, those who give such gifts, do so in gratitude of some past shady deal or in anticipation of some undeserved favor in the future. When the President and his wife accepted very expensive gifts from all sorts of characters, including some whose sources of wealth are "unknown", during the naming ceremony of their fourth child in 1989 they were simply being corrupt.

The rush by transnational corporations, traditional rulers and the wealthy in the country to present gifts to the President and his wife under the guise of presenting gifts to the new born baby, was merely an excuse to strengthen ties and ensure that they were noticed against the future. By promoting officers who had formally retired from the military, the President was equally abusing his office and power and using public funds to resolve personal contradictions. After all Domkat Bali and Augustus Aikhomu, who are no longer serving officers of the Nigeria army and navy are going to collect allowances and exercise power from respective new positions and ranks of full general.[53] In today's Nigeria corruption has become a problem with implications for development planning, power positions and balances, the constitution of civil society and the future 0 democracy.

Today, virtually no Nigerian believes in hard work or that hard work pays. It used to be said in the very early years of political independence that "honesty is the best policy. " Mammy wagons and buses carried this inscription and many

Nigerians believed in it. Today, what they would like to carry is "Honesty is a stupid policy". As Seyi Olu Awofeso has noted, "corruption which started with the inception of Nigeria as a sovereign state, has now bred a mentality of contempt for long-term work and investment. The common image of the (new rich), governor, secretaries and so on, could well have stuck to the brain of new born babes".[54] Secondly, with corruption in virtually every nook and corner of the society, development planning is reduced to one huge joke. Public funds are embezzled before they are even allocated and because corruption has eaten to deep into the body politic, there are no mechanisms for accountability, plan discipline, monitoring and efficiency.

Implementation of development Plans and projects is measured mainly by the ability to spend allocation not by the ability to complete projects to the satisfaction of the people. As Seyi Awofeso notes, the "spill-over effects" of corruption "are total chaos in service sectors of the economy: transport, health and education run shoe-string budgets, since most of the stolen funds have been spirited out and invested in ventures overseas". He concludes that the situation is so serious that given the seeming "uncontrollable effects of corruption... no, government can again control funds in the hands of corruptly self-enriching officials and hanger-ons".[55] Dan Agbese of the Newswatch captures very well the implications of widespread and almost officially sanctioned corruption for national development and economic recovery when he notes that,

> The "c" word again. Corruption. Or the "f" word: fraud. Two sides of the ruinous coin. They are the killer words, the rapier in the soft underbelly of all good intention, all good plans, all good projects. They dog man's every step not because they are evil but because they are the smartest means employed by the smart people to reduce the distance between their present and their ultimate ambition - wealth and the good life. No thanks to them, good plans go wrong. No thanks to them, bad plans displace good plans and the former are implemented against sound, sane and expert advice. The white elephant projects multiply ad infinitum... There may be no getting away. How, indeed, can there? Often the brain that thinks of a cure for the headache is the same brain that brings up what causes the headache in the first place.[56]

Third, by turning a blind eye to corruption, rehabilitating corrupt a discredited persons and encouraging corruption by practicing it, Nigerian leaders have over the decades tended to show that corruption is alright. Nigerians are no longer afraid to defraud the state. In fact, it is believed that to defraud the State is a good thing. So, under the Babangida regime as well as Abachas, "when there is some misdemeanor, especially that involving finagling with public funds, we seek to convey the impression that what has taken place is no more than a slight breach of procedure rather than a malevolent act of stealing. Where once they would have been charged with corruption or corruptly enriching themselves, offending public officers or rather those who draw attention to themselves are now presented as having committed the offence of misappropriation of funds"[57] Fourth, corruption has contributed in a major way to the country's internal and external debt profiles. Money stolen is stashed away in foreign banks or squandered on unproductive ventures. A recent report showed that "some foreign bank vaults are bursting with $33 billion (N260 billion) stashed away by some 'Wealthy Nigerians".[58] The report, prepared by the Morgan Trust Guarantee Bank of New York also showed that "rich Nigerians have accounts in almost every bank and in almost all countries of the world".[59]

It is interesting to note that this figure of $33 billion represents only a tiny fraction of what Nigerians have lodged with foreign banks. Even more interesting is the fact that the Contra Bank of Nigeria(CBN) announced in October 1990 that the country's foreign debt stood at $33 billion at the end of October 1990.[60] The classic case of Zaire where stolen money in foreign banks equaled the foreign debt profile was replayed. Fifth, since those found guilty of corruption are not punished, if anything they are praised, Nigerians now accept corruption as a way of life and as the only way to get things done and to climb the social ladder. By appointing disgraced and discredited persons to positions of responsibility, the government was directly legitimizing corruption and institutionalizing it within its structures and institutions. The attitude of Nigerian leaders to acts of corruption forced Professor Adeoye Lambo who served for years at the World Health Organization to lament that " when one takes a serious look at the behavior of Nigerian leaders, one cannot escape the conclusion that they are mentally ill".[61] Sixthly, the majority of Nigerians have become corrupt and now accept the reality that they can get nothing done without offering bribes. It is not true that Nigerians are by nature corrupt. Rather, under conditions of deprivation, neglect, repression, poverty, unemployment, disillusionment, poor leadership, manipulation and general harassment, they have come to include corruption as part of the numerous strategies of survival in a very harsh world. Seventh, wealth is now equated with power. With the Babangida and Abacha regime's attack on labor, progressive scholars and professionals, trade unionists and students, and their prohibition from the political processes, the political terrain has now been abandoned to thieves, disgraced politicians, retired generals, tradition rulers and other characters who have historically subscribed to the philosophy of "money politics."

It is no wonder that the content and direction of the current political process is interpreted by the government and the politics actors as an avenue to accumulate capital in the name of promoting democracy.

The eight point has to do with the way in which the delegitimization and weakening of the state has increased with the deepening of corruption. No one trusts the state, its agents and agencies. Its policies carry no legitimacy its rules and regulations are not obeyed. Its word carries no command and its institutions are treated and related to as structures of oppression and exploitation. How can such a state structure promote self-reliance, discipline, mobilization, accountability, harmony and recovery from political and economic crisis? Furthermore, ninth, it must be noted with all seriousness that corruption has been the cause of several coups and counter-coups d'etat in Nigeria. From Nzeogwu, through Murtala to Buhari/Idiagbon, the issue of corruption has remained constant as the main cause of military intervention in the political process. The April 22 1990 coup led by Major Gideon Orka cited corruption as one main reason for its attempt to seize power from Ibrahim Babangida:

> I, Major Gideon Orka, wish to happily inform you of the successful ousting of the dictatorial, corrupt, drug baronish, evil men, sadistic, deceitful, homosexually centred, prodigalistic, unpatriotic administration of General Ibrahim Badamasi Babangida. We have equally commenced their trials for unabated corruption, mismanagement of the national economy... This exercise will not be complete without purging corrupt public officials and recovering all ill-gotten wealth since the days of the oil boom... We are extremely determined to recover all ill-gotten wealth back to the public treasury for the use of the masses of our people."[62]

Corruption is certain to remain a major cause of military coups even if plotters are not sincere in their reasons, they will continue to use it as an excuse. The Babangida regime did not help matters in any way by elevating corruption into an art and the same is true of Abacha regime. Finally, tenth, the primitive accumulation of "empowered" the bourgeoisie to an extent where they now live and obey the law. Jato Thompson has noted that the "lavish life-style of state belies their normal salaries".[63] The former Chief of General Staff, Augustus Aikhomu, in one of the very rare occasions in which he spoke against corruption confessed in 1989, that "corruption is now said to be organized and endemic some local government areas... where council members reportedly demanded for gratification from contractors as pre-condition for the award of contracts".[64] Olu Awogbemila has also argued that the structural adjustment program which he brands a "season of SAP sadness" has in spite of the pain "turned into a period of joy for some Nigerians" only because they engaged in acts of corruption and got away with such acts.[65]

The implication of the situations highlighted above is that, though illegal and quite unorthodox, the acts of corruption has created "several formidable centers of power, capable of stalemating the interests of Nigeria's Federal government". Awofeso believes that in the very near "future, this may become Nigeria's next nettlesome political problem"[66] With billionaires and millionaires who have no regard for the law, who believe that they can get what they want at any time, who rely on manipulation and the intimidation of the poor in the political processes and who have very limited interests in production, the future of politics and capitalist development in Nigeria cannot be said to bright. Many members of the bourgeois class have begun to recruit their own body guards and security forces, several are getting top military and police officers their pay rolls, forging alternative political and economic networks in and outside the country outside, sometimes in conflict with government laid down lea and regulations and are beginning to map out their own political agenda irrespective of whatever programs the military regime might have on its political program.

Without doubt, this will be one fundamental obstacle to the stability, growth, development and recovery of the economy in the next decade.

NOTES

1) Lateef Jakande, Former Civilian Governor of Lagos State, delivering the Third Dele Giwa Memorial Lecture. Quoted in *Newswatch* (November 5, 1990).
2) Government by the Thief Under IBB". Leaflet distributed during the 19th-SAP Demonstration, Port Harcourt.
3) Eme Ekekwe, *Class and State In Nigeria* (Lagos and London: Longman, 1986, p.113
4) Ekekwe, *Class and State*,... op. cit., p.113.
5) ibid
6) ibid, p.114.
7) Sully Abu, "Boy George", *The Guardian* on Sunday (Lagos) (February 17 1991), p.A7.
8) ibid.
9) Quoted from "Gowon's Men Probed", *The Analyst* (Kaduna, Nigeria), (July, 1986), p.16.
10) Another Blockbuster", Review of Arthur Nzeribe, Nigeria: Seven Years After Shehu Shagari(London:Kilimanjaro Publishing House Limited, 1990) in *Africa Concord* (Nigeria)(September 24, 1990)
11) See Eddie Madunagu, Nigeria: the Economy and the People - The Political Economy of State Robbery and its Popular Democratic Negation(London: New Beacon, 1984); "How They Live, How We Die", *The Analyst* Vol.2 (7) (1987).
12) ibid.
13) "Who Will Probe Babangida?", *Newbreed* (Lagos) (I October, 1990).
14) ibid, p.11.
15) See "Drops of Oil on Agreements: Idem Commission in Cross River Uncovers Irregularities in Lease Agreement of Oil Palm Estates", *Newswatch* (June 11, 1990)
16) ibid.
17) ibid (emphasis added).
18) "Corruption a Nigerian?", *African Concord* (26 March 1990), p.30.
19) "Corruption a Nigerian?"., op. cit., p.31.

20) "Corruption, A Nigerian?", African Concord(26 March 1990), p.30. See Governors are Corrupt - Madaki's Insider Account", *African Concord* (26 March, 1990).
21) ibid, p.12.
22) "Million N Tenement rate Ripoff in Ogun State - N4.4 million Involved", *Probe Magazine* (Lagos) (December 15, 1988).
23) "A Fight Without End", *The African Guardian* (August 27, 1990), p.23.
24) ibid. See also "Who Will Probe Babangida?", op. cit.
25) ibid.
26) See "Battle of Nerves: Ex-Governor of Anambra State Locked in a Dispute with the incumbent over Land", *African Concord* (6 August, 1990).
27) "An Era of Scandals", *African Concord* (11 February 1991), p.29.
28) ibid.
29) ibid, p.30
30) "An Era of Scandals", op. cit., p.34.
31)."The Boats George Bought", *African Concord* (11 February 1990).
32) Femi Macaulay, "The Sack of Sirajo" *African Concord*(6 August, 1990).
33) "Corruption a Nigerian?", op. cit., p.31.
34) "Nigeria: Fake Debt", *West Africa* (7-13 January 1991).
35) "Ups and Downs: Punished", *African Concord*(27 August 1990), P.52.
36) "School Principals Punished", *African Concord* (27 August, 1990), p.40
37) "A Hundred Million Naira Riddle", *African Concord*(18 June, 1990), p.40.
38) "From the States: Bendel", *West Africa* (3-9 December, 1990).
39) "Crime: NI.5 m Media Theft: court fixes October 19" Newbreed
(August 20, 1990)p.46
40) "Nigeria: 1992-Nzeribe's Fears", *African Concord* (24 September 1990)p.28
41) Today(Kaduna) (16 October 1988).
42) Quoted in "Corruption, A Nigerian?", op. cit., p.33.
43) "Corruption, a Nigerian?", op. cit., p.33.
44) ibid.
45) The discussion of the Auditor-General's 1988 Report was based on reports in *African Concord* (26 March 1990).
46) See "Tam in Trouble", African Concord (22 October 1990); "The Trials of David West", *African Concord* (24 September 1990) and "Minister Had President's Mandate", *African Concord* (22 October 1990).

47) See Victor Omuabor, "The Crusader Thinks of Exile - After an Attempt on Her Life, Calabar Based anti-corruption Crusader, Grace Eyo-Ita Contemplates Leaving.Nigeria", *African Concord* (27 August, 1990).

48) "The People's Verdict: Nigerians Score Babangida's Third Year - It's not Easy Assessment", *African Concord* (2nd September, 1988), p.13.

49) "Corruption, A Nigerian?", op cit., p.32.

50) ibid.

51) Uzor Mazim Uzoatu, "Reaping the Negative way", *This Week* (April 2 1990), p.15

52) Quoted in "Corruption, A Nigerian?", op. cit., p.32.

53) See "Why Did IBB Do It - Riddles Emerge as Nigeria's Leader Promotes Two Retired Officers as Generals", *African Concord* (22 October 1990).

54) Seyi Olu Awofeso, "Decades of Nightmare", *African Concord* (8 October 1990), p.28.

55) ibid, p.29.

56) Dan Agbese, "Jogging in the Dump", *Newswatch* (September 3, 1990), p.1

57) Sully Abu, "Boy George", op. cit.

58) "Nigerians Have $33bn in Foreign Accounts", *National Concord* (August 1, 1990).

59) ibid

60) See "Nigeria's Debt Stands at $33 billion", *The Punch* (October 17, 1990).

61) Adeoye Lambo quoted in "Seyi Awofeso, Decades of Nightmare", op. cit., p.29.

62) Coup Broadcast Statement by Major Gideon Orka, April 22, 1990. Full text is in published in *Newswatch* (May 7 1990).

63) Jato Thompson, "Corruption the Trigger", *New African* (June 1990), p.12.

64) "Corruption, A Nigerian", op. cit., p.32.

65) "Reaping the Negative Way", *This Week* (April 2, 1990), p.15.

66) Seyi Awofeso, "Decades of Nightmare", op. cit., p.29.

INDEX